Connections
Reflections of A Spiritual Journey

**BY
ROBBIE BRONNER**

Connections

Copyright © 2007 by Robbie Bronner

All rights reserved. No part of this book may be reproduced or transmitted in any form or by any means without written permission of the author.

DEDICATION

I dedicate this book to my late husband, Nathaniel Bronner and to my late son, Darrow Bronner for being the best part of my life.

ACKNOWLEDGMENTS

Thank you, God our Father - Jesus Christ - Holy Spirit, for enabling and designating me to write this book.

All Scripture quotations are taken from the King James Version of the Bible.

Data Entry	Mamie Bell, Michaelle Smith, and Gloria Locke
Data Organization	Delores Harmon
Manuscript Editor	Sandy at Edit911.com
Layout and Proofing	Shelli Davis and Britte Blair
Cover	Gary Crawford and Nathaniel Bronner, Jr.
Sketching	Felida Neily
Photographers	Reggie Anderson, Dwight Cook, and Dwayne "Snapper" Mack

My Cheerleaders
  All my sons and their wives
  Prentice and Maxine Foster
  My mother, Ivester Rutland
  Ann Mitchell (Prayer Partner)
  Evangelist Freda Slaughter (Friend)
  Janet Wallace
  Harriet Pitt
  Shirley Singh Cooksey
  Mary Rhoden
  Dr. Rose Sloan
  Barbara Smith
  Rev. Dr. Meachum – St. Louis
  Rev. Jackie Reed – St. Louis

Aldoris Hudson – St. Louis
Word of Faith Cathedral
Word of Faith Love Center
Word of Faith Light and Joy
The Ark of Salvation
The Bronner family
Forsyth Dialysis Center
St. Luke AME Church – Forsyth, Georgia
Melvin Lawrence - Forsyth Older American Council
Mr. N. T. Lindsey
Bronner Bros. Company Employees
The Lynn Valley Community and the Peyton Chalet
Dr. Julia Glass and Family
Wheat Street Baptist Church
Barbara Jean Shannon
Julia Mae Tanner
Roxie Redding
Mr. and Mrs. Larry Evans
Mr. and Mrs. Charles Wilder
Mr. and Mrs. James Henry Moore
Mr. and Mrs. Marcus Whitehead
Dorothy Jones
Mary Robert Slaughter
Areatha Neal
Mr. and Mrs. David Sewell
Brittanica Stewart
Mr. and Mrs. James Maddox
The Monroe/Hendricks Family

PROLOGUE

Waiting on God While He Is Waiting on Me

I found myself in a situation where circumstances were allowed to rob me of doing what I had begun to do and that was write a book. I thank God for planting angels along the way to guide and instruct me when I moved off course or became passive in my endeavors. Truly, I had spoken, "I will just wait for the inspiration of the Holy Spirit to come upon me and overwhelm me to write the book." I just did not feel the divine inspiration to write; the thoughts were not coming. I had to learn that God had given us experiences and a daily walk of life as we traveled along life's journey in order to pass on to others just how we made it.

What were the hurdles we had to overcome? How did we overcome them? In 1996, returning home from a three-week stay as a caretaker for my ill mother, I was in my comfort zone. Near the end of the day, I heard the doorbell ringing. My grandson, Darrow, Jr., was visiting with me and yelled, "I'll answer the door." I am sure he thought it was his mom or dad coming to pick him up, but it was not. To my surprise, there stood a gentleman. I stepped outside. This gentleman was looking for the owner of the house diagonally behind my house. He said, "I went to the house to the left and right of the house diagonally behind you, seeking the owner of the house between them. Somehow someone directed me to your house and said you knew the person who owns the house." I admitted I knew the person who owned it, but it was now in possession of the bank. He stood there with no attempt to leave and somehow another conversation developed.

We talked about many different things and ended with my telling him I had to write a book on how God brought us through to where we are now. At that point, it was as though he exploded from the inside: "Write the book! Write the book! Write the book! People need to know how God prospered your family and how your six sons were developed." He literally began to preach to me about Jesus, who came to live the Word and show us the way. "As you live, God wants you to show the way you handled difficulties and obstacles as they invaded your life. He wants a book that shows 'the human part' and 'the God part.'" The human part, he explained, was "Jesus hungered"; but as He brought forth the God part, He said, "I am the bread of life."

I exclaimed, "Oh, I've got it! Just tell the story. Surely, the story will be filled with weaknesses and strengths." I thought to myself for a moment, looked at him, smiled, and said, "You did not come here to inquire about a house and the ownership, but you came to further me along my journey of writing the book."

He laughed, "I am not thinking about that house; I could care less about it. You write your book. If I have to come to this door every day and ring your doorbell, I will do it until you write the book. A nation is waiting for the book; women are waiting, and men are waiting. You must write the book."

I solemnly promised to begin again to write the book and started that very night. He insisted, if I spent just one hour a day, I would get the book written. I assured him he had been an angel sent by God to stir me up and inspire me with the significance of writing. He ended by saying, "Once the book is finished, it will speak to your children, your grandchildren, and even unto generations to come as a testimony and as eyes to watch over them." THE BOOK WILL SPEAK!

The Naming of the Book

There was a knock on my kitchen door. Peeping from the door panel covering the glass door, I saw my son, Nathaniel. I answered, "Just a minute, please," as I rushed to the front door to disengage the alarm system. Rushing back to the kitchen door, I realized he wasn't there. He had fled, but left at the door was a rolled paper. Hurriedly, I sat down to see what he had placed at my door. One thought was that it was a picture of his new product, Miracle 2000®. A second thought came that it was some material for me to proofread. Just in a second, I gently removed two pieces of masking tape that secured the most gorgeous, meaningful, and thought-provoking cover designed for my book.

I had been wrestling with a title for the book and here it was all completed. I was being forced into writing this book. Dr. Myles Monroe says, "When you say yes to the Lord, God will cause the camels in the East to come unto you bearing gifts." Tears filled my eyes. I picked up the telephone and called Nathaniel. The voice on the other end said, "Yes." He knew it was his mother. I simply said, "Speak. I want to know amid your busy schedule, how did you think of designing a book cover and what prompted you to do it?"

He was silent.

I asked, "What is going on?"

With a gentle smile in his voice the answer came, "You have a story to tell. Tell it and people will be blessed."

"A profile of my face is in the cloud on the right of the birds, and to the left is the rear profile." I really felt that only I could see these images and attribute them to me. The light from the heavens seemed to illuminate my face also on the cover. Later, I discovered it was a hand; an African guest in my home saw it and pointed that out to me. I was sure that only I could see the abstract of the profile. It was there to bear witness to me that this is my book cover. I accepted that thought, gave thanks to God Almighty, and played the tape, *Praise Jehovah*.

To God Be the Glory!

A Letter from a Daughter

November 18, 2000

Mother,

I don't understand why, but I cannot sleep peacefully. I just keep hearing, "She needs to finish that book," over and over again! I am not saying who is saying it; however, the thought won't let me rest. It's like I am here in bed and I keep hearing reasons for me to tell you to finish writing. I'm sure you have been charged up and boosted enough from your sons, and I don't mean to add any more pressure. I just want to go to sleep. All I know is the wealth of knowledge you have within you needs to be down on paper. Yes, for the outside world to read and know you and what you have accomplished through (the strength of) Christ, but mainly because our children must read and have an account of their wonderful history. Just as Abraham wrote the history on his staff, passed it down to his children, and made sure it was taught to each generation about God by whom all they had was given, so must you pass the staff of the Bronner heritage on to your children and your children's children. You are that cornerstone that the builders rejected. They doubted your strength and ability to hold up the foundation. The same cornerstone in every church gives the history of that place for all to read and know who and what people God used from generation to generation.

> *You are that pillar to the Bronner name.*
> *All that your sons are…you prayed them.*
> *All that your family is….you made them.*
> *All that will go to heaven…Jesus saved them.*
> *All the history to give our children…you gave them…*

Our children must know what had to transpire in order for them to be here so they can know who they are…It is said if you don't know your history; you are destined to repeat it. From the little history that I've heard about the 12 stones of the Bronner family, just the one stone I know, his history is WORTH knowing, memorizing, and repeating. Please finish it so you can tell it personally, as Abraham, Isaac, and Jacob did to their children and their children to their children and so on. As I said, I know you have been charged and boosted (probably) too many times. I just kept hearing that you are the cornerstone to this family and what you hold is essential to the foundation. Maybe I can sleep now! I love you and take this for what it's worth, a grain of salt or a pillar of fire!

Your Daughter,

Stephanie

P.S. I don't know WHAT the book is about. I just wrote what came out. John 13:15 1:09 a.m.

For I have given you an example, that you should do as I have done to you. (John 13:15)

TABLE OF CONTENTS

**Our Path of Life Through
the First Five Books of the Bible: (The TORAH)
Genesis, Exodus, Leviticus, Numbers, Deuteronomy**

ACKNOWLEDGEMENTS..v

PROLOGUE:...vii

INTRODUCTION: THE MANDATE...1

| *Our Genesis* | Birth to 20 years of age | Birthing is the beginning of anything. Take it personally; you are young, at home, nurtured by your parents up to twenty years of age. Your dependency is on parents/family and God. This is where you are taught of the Lord. |

CHAPTER 1: OUR BEGINNING..3
- The Bronner Lineage..4
- My Mother on a Mission...10
- The Rutland Lineage..16
- Remembering Papa..19
- My Parents..21

| *Our Exodus* | 20 – 30 years of age | You're going out, leaving home as a teenager, and going off to college. You're taking on job experiences, marriage and children. You begin to practice what you have been taught. |

CHAPTER 2: OUR MARRIAGE..25
- Moving On Up The Road......................................28
- The Ark of the Covenant......................................30
- Rooms in the House..34
  - The Front Porch...34
  - The Birthing Chamber..................................35
- Leaving The Basement: Going to Get Married..........49

CHAPTER 3: THE BEAUTY OF MARRIAGE..........................51
- Keeping a Marriage Fresh..................................52
- A Visitation From the Holy Spirit........................53
- Marriage: Resolution of Conflict and Anger...........53
- A Spirit of Jealousy Through Vain Imaginations.......58
- Family Finances in Tight Times..........................61
- Our House Through Psalm 23............................64
- Our Pointers to Strengthen Your Marriage............65

CHAPTER 4: BOYS' EARLY YEARS......................................67
- How Did We Rear Six Wonderful Sons?...............67
- The Teenage Stage..71
- Dale's Walk With God......................................72
- The Meeting of a Prayer Partner........................75
- How God Guided Us in Saving Our Children.........78
- Prophesy Over The Children.............................79
- Observing The Children...................................80

| *Our Leviticus* | 20 – 40 years of age | You are working in conjunction with the Exodus because you go out with the laws, rules, and regulations of God as you practice life's adventures. This period also embraces the wilderness experience where you either die or come out victorious. |

CHAPTER 5: YOUTHFUL EPISODES..91
- Bernard's Early Life's Lesson...............................91
- Darrow's Early Life's Lesson...............................93
- How We Coped When Our Two Oldest Sons Delved Into the Music Industry and Later the Movie Industry...94

CHAPTER 6: THE LESSONS OF THE HAND........................ 97
- Walking By Faith 97
- The Five Fingers 98
- A Return to the Front Porch for Retirement..............99

CHAPTER 7: SONS SEEKING THEIR BRIDES......................101
- Dale and Nina...101
- Bernard and Sheila...103
- Darrow and Jane..105
- Charles and Traci...109
- Nathaniel and Stacey..111
- James and Stephanie..115
- Rules I Must Obey..119
- The Household Mission Statement........................120

Our Numbers

40 to 50 years of age

This is where your experience from the wilderness (the battleground **where you live or die**) will now demand you to practice the noble and good things you have mastered. One day you'll find yourself waking up to the fact that you are now 50 years old and accountability is asking how you spent those 50 years.

CHAPTER 8: THE BUSINESS..123
- BB International Beauty Show.........................126
  - An Historical Overview...............................126
  - A Typical Experience at a BB International Fashion Show..127
- Preparing the Next Generation to Take Over.........129
- The Institution of BB Continuity......................129
- Accountability Asks: "What Have You Done With the Talents I Have Given You?......................130
  - First Generation...131
  - Second Generation......................................132
- The Changing of the Guard............................133

CHAPTER 9: HEALTH AND PHYSICAL ACTIVITIES..........141
- Cottonwood Hot Springs................................142
- Sins of the Heart: Jealousy............................143
- The Lying Spirit...145

CHAPTER 10: EDUCATION..149
- A, B, Cs - Always Be Certified From God............149
- College Graduates..150
- World Mission: Bearing Precious Seed................152

Our Deuteronomy   50 years of age and onward   You are not the student anymore but the teacher; and you must now teach all you have learned from generation to generation.

CHAPTER 11: THE MISSING LINK.....................................155
- The Mighty Oak Tree....................................155
- Grandma's Boot Camp..................................156
- The Story of the Hand Tree............................159
- Grandchildren: Twenty-Nine and Growing...........162
- Grandchildren's Destiny Statements..................163
- Our Fourth Generation..................................166

CHAPTER 12: ACCOUNTABILITY..167
- An Inheritance...……....167
- Blessing of the Sons..……....169

CHAPTER 13: LETTERS FROM THE SONS..........................171

CHAPTER 14: PEACE IN THE STORM................................183

THE DREAM..186

THE DREAM MANIFESTED...…...................................….187

THE LEGACY STATEMENT..188
- From the Father to the Sons.............................….....188
- Grandmamma Robbie to the Grandchildren.........189

AN INVITATION TO THE ULTIMATE CONNECTION..........190

CHRIST IS COMING..191

PICTURES...193

Introduction

THE MANDATE

Connection: Something that joins or binds two or more parts, to make into one.

A divine mandate has been placed upon me to share how my husband, Nathaniel H. Bronner, Sr. and I were able to rear six sons while building a multimillion dollar business enterprise. As you might imagine, it was not easy. It took a lot of prayer, an enormous amount of hard work and repeated withdrawals from a well of wisdom. We relied heavily upon the strong value system of our ancestors and their tremendous faith in God. We recognized all of these factors as we acknowledged many victories. In spite of many obstacles and challenges in life, we remained intact as a solid family unit.

God deserves supreme credit for everything that we have achieved. It is because of Him that we are able to share our accomplishments. My late husband was the vessel through whom God poured the wisdom and leadership to build our family. I was his helpmeet. I was blessed to walk beside him. He was the visionary. We walked together to implement the vision. By being an obedient and a yielded vessel, I have realized abundance, joy, and fulfillment as a wife and mother.

We will be forever grateful for the memory of Arthur E. Bronner, Sr., who was my husband's business partner at the time we began the business endeavors. He remained with the company beyond my husband's death and served until his body became frail. He was a true watchman upon the wall. Arthur was an integral part of our beginning, thus the mandate requires acknowledgement of his lifelong contribution.

There are those who came before me who helped both of us to continue on the journey. You will read about some of these individuals in this book. There are also those who, at the present time, search for answers and direction as to how to live a victorious life, to seek mates, to rear families, to provide for them, to build businesses, and to navigate the waters of life. My sole purpose in writing this book is to reach out to this audience and share the matchless power found in connecting God, family, and business!

I especially carry a burden for the preservation of the family unit as God intended. *Connections* represents the response to the call upon me to draw from the well of waters over the years and share how our family grew, developed, and persevered in spite of whatever came our way. By reading our story, I pray that you will find answers that you need.

There are those who often ask the question, "How did you and Mr. Bronner rear six wonderful sons?" The response is, "It's a process." That process will be revealed throughout this book. There are also wonderful stories of youthful experiences and the development of unique personalities in each of the six sons as they began their individual journeys.

It is my prayer that, by the time I have relived our journey in this book, you will discover all the connections necessary to reach your life's goals. I invite you now to travel to small Southern towns, to big cities in America, across the Atlantic to Europe, and to the Holy Lands of the Bible. In one way or the other, they all play vital parts in the shaping of the Bronner story. They are all connected!

May God bless you,

Robbie Bronner

Chapter 1: Our Beginning

Emerging from the rural south in a place called Kelly, Georgia, located 60 miles southeast of Atlanta in Jasper County, my husband was empowered early to dream, build, motivate, lead, and pioneer. Little did he know that his destiny included national recognition.

There was just so much about country living that city life could not duplicate. Growing up in the country, my husband lived in a natural classroom for human bonding: experimenting barefoot up and down country roads, growing vegetables in the yard, and drawing water from a well. There were also the special aromas of Southern cooking from the houses, mingling with fresh honeysuckle and rosebushes on the outside. The country was a special place, a wonderful paradise in which to begin life.

Life was not always as easy as the term paradise would signal because it was here in the South that some women had to tie their babies on their backs as they picked cotton or tilled long rows in the field. They returned to humble homes and cooking pots that had simmered slowly all day. Surely by now, they were all tired. Late home arrivals in the evening represented the beginning of another shift after an already hard day's work. Still, they bent over washtubs, cleaned the houses, and addressed the needs of their children. These were the days prior to birth control, so there was usually a house full of children who required constant attention.

The plight of men in the rural South was no better than that of the women in most instances. They, too, worked from sunup to sundown and returned home to children who needed their fathers.

Nathaniel, whose parents had eleven children, was one such child born into similar circumstances. Practically from infancy, he worked in the field and helped his mother with chores around the house. One can understand how at age sixteen his siblings began to leave the house in the country and not look back! Some of them found refuge in the big city of Atlanta at the Atlanta Daily World (the nation's oldest African American newspaper). In fact, his eldest brother, Clinton, became the circulation manager. This opened the door for all the other siblings to find work there as they attended Clark College and Morehouse College. Some of them later migrated to Cleveland, Chicago, and Washington, D.C. Little did they know they were being geographically positioned to participate in and guard a dream attached to destiny.

Standing l to r: Daniel Weslow, Charles, Nathaniel, Clinton, Person, Arthur.
Seated l to r: Emma, Emma J., James, Juanita, Malaral, Not pictured are Cottrell, Indus, and Catherine.

The Bronner Lineage

Nathaniel's parents, James and Emma Bronner, birthed eleven children from their marriage union. The children were Clinton, Person, Charles, Emma, James Cottrell, Nathaniel, Arthur, Indus Doyle, Malaral, Daniel Weslow, and Juanita. They also reared Emma's niece, Catherine.

As a part of the same root system, I have traced the branches to reveal how they each prospered, coming from the same taproot as Nathaniel and Arthur.

Clinton, the eldest of the Bronner siblings, was influential in leading the younger brothers to Cleveland, Ohio, and later back to Atlanta. He became the circulation manager at the Atlanta Daily World newspaper and later graduated from Clark College. He married Elease Harrison, a teacher in the Atlanta Public School System. Their union produced one child, Lena. Like her father, Lena graduated from Clark College and married Enoch Webb. This union produced one child, Enoch, Jr. Enoch Jr. married Melanie. They are both employed as Fulton County tax assessors and have two children, Alexandra and Enoch III.

Person, the second son, migrated to Chicago and opened Bronner Brothers' Grocery Store. Later, he worked for the Atlantic Railroad as a sleeping car porter. He married Louise and they had no children. Later, Person united with Cottrell and Daniel, his two brothers in Chicago, and organized Bronner Brothers' Mid-West Distribution Center, where they distributed beauty supply products.

Charles, the third sibling, followed Clinton to Cleveland to work in a rubber plant. This lasted for a short time. He returned to Atlanta and graduated from Clark College and later became a circulation manager at the Atlanta Daily World. Charles had a Kirby vacuum cleaner business in Washington, D.C., and he also sold hair care products in his store. He married Jeannetta Alexander, who was a nurse. This union produced one child, Charlene, who became an attorney and married J. Thomas and had one child, Jamila.

Emma, the first girl born among the three brothers, attended Apex Beauty College. This also inspired Nathaniel to attend Apex Beauty College to learn the trade. (Nathaniel sold beauty supply products in front of Emma's Beauty Shop. BANG! Here come the Bronner Brothers selling beauty supply products. Nathaniel always used the phrase when referring to his start, "Born out of a beauty shop!") Emma married Henderson Lewis, and they had no children.

James Cottrell, the fifth child, graduated from Clark College. He later became a certified custom upholsterer and interior designer. He established his own business, Bronner Upholstery & Repair Service, where he served the Chicago area suburbs. Cottrell married Annice, and they had two daughters, Anita and Bernice.

Nathaniel, my husband, was the sixth child and "the Dreamer." He was motivated by a sign that read, "Beauty: The Depression-Proof Business," at the end of the Big Depression, which ignited the fire that propelled him into the beauty industry.

Arthur, the seventh child, also followed Clinton to Cleveland and worked in the dry cleaning business. Nathaniel beckoned Arthur home to Atlanta to help him with the beauty supply business. Arthur attended Blayton Business School in Atlanta. He was Executive Vice President of Bronner Bros. and worked side by side with his brother. He married Theodora McKinney, and they had two sons, Arthur II (deceased as an infant) and Arthur III. Arthur, Sr. later married Ann Wright after the death of Theodora. Arthur III married Jennette, and this union produced one child, Tamiko. He later adopted Elisha, Jennette's son. Arthur III is now married to Brenda Roberts.

Indus Doyle, the eighth child, transitioned at sixteen years old.

Malaral, the second daughter and the ninth sibling, graduated from Washington High School in Atlanta. She began as Nathaniel's first secretary for the Bronner Bros. business located outside of their sister's beauty shop and sold hair care products and fruit. Malaral later married Willie Glover; and from this union, three children were born: William James and a set of twins, Calvin and Carolyn. Malaral sold products from a little black bag and today her son Calvin is also a beauty salon route salesman for Bronner Bros. Company in Atlanta.

Daniel Weslow, the tenth sibling, worked 34 years for the U.S. Postal Service. Daniel was Vice President of the Midwest Division of Bronner Bros. Company. He married Ruby; and from their union, four children were born: Gwethalyn, Daniel Jr., Michael, and Pamela.

Juanita, the eleventh (and the baby) started attending high school in Philadelphia and returned to Atlanta to finish high school and to attend Clark College. She studied the "Hair-Weev New Invention System" by Christina Jenkins of Cleveland and became a renowned Hair-Weev technician, consultant, and teacher. She set up the school of Hair-Weev and was director of the hair styling contests in the beauty shows. Juanita was the retail store manager for the Bronner Bros. Beauty Salon and Retail Cosmetic Center, located at the Mall West-End in Atlanta. She was married to Roscoe Garmon and had two sons, Reginald and Richard. Reginald married Lisa Kilpatrick, and they have three children: Rachael, Brianna, and Reginald III. Reginald is pastor of Word of Faith Love Center on Ben Hill Road in Atlanta.

Catherine graduated from Clark College and was manager of the Bronner Bros. warehouse, renamed BB Shipping Department. Catherine worked every phase of the business. She married George Render; and from their union, three children were born: Georgette, George Roland, and Gerald. Georgette transitioned at age 13. Roland is married to Sherri Bailey, and they have two sons, George III and Jared. Gerald is married to Traci Blackshear, and they have two children, Gerald, Jr. and Brooke Catherine.

These are the **twelve stones** of the Bronner family. We are now teaching the next two generations.

Being accountable to the **past** is relevant to our **present**, which connects us to our **future**. There is a Chinese proverb that says, **"To forget one's ancestors is to be a brook without a source, a tree without a root."**

The Original Bronner Bros. Beauty Supply Company

(Nathaniel H. Bronner and Arthur E. Bronner)

Nathaniel Seeks a Wife And God Prepares Me To Receive My Husband

And the Bible says, "He who finds a wife finds a good thing." (Prov. 18:22 NKJV)

My Mother on a Mission

The summer of 1954 found my mother, Ivester Rutland, doing the thing she loved best—attending to the needs of her family. A classic Proverbs 31 woman, she rose early and attended to daily household management chores. One of the immediate concerns at this point was finding a suitable husband for me, her youngest daughter. Surveying the "pickings" in our small rural town, she initiated the single conversation that began to shape my destiny. She said to me, "I am sending you to summer school to find your husband. There is no one in Forsyth for you to marry."

There was an old adage that if you came out of college without a husband you were doomed to become an old maid. There was nothing factual in this belief, but girls passed it on as gospel truth. We played the card game Old Maid, hoping that this would be as close as we would come to realizing the plight of a lonely and unspoken-for woman. Fortunately, my sister was attending Atlanta University, completing work on a master's degree in biology. As I prepared to enter a whole new world, the last words my mother shared before I departed were, "Robbie, hold on to your purse. You are going to the big city and people will snatch your purse." I assured her that I would be responsible. There was one last yell: "Don't go out at night without your sister because it is a big and dangerous city." To this day, I remember her words. I have tried to be careful, to be responsible, and to watch out for anyone who would take unfair advantage of me.

Within a few days, the two of us, giggly and cute, were off to school. Although Maxine was only a year and nine months older than me, Maxine's mind and maturity were ten years ahead of mine. My mother had made a wise decision and had left me in good hands: Maxine acted like the mother and I had sense enough to act like her child.

As you'll note, I will frequently use illustrations from the Bible. It was in the book of Ruth that I found the example of a giving and caring husband. He would provide the example of a model husband. I called him "my Boaz."

Boaz was a man of great wealth from the town of Bethlehem. His life was the classic example of sacrifice and faithfulness. He was a man of substantial means. He was rich and was the God-sent husband to Ruth. God blessed her life of sacrifice and dedication in connection with Boaz, who incidentally happened to be a great deal older than she.

Little did I know that, as we arrived on the tree-lined lawns of Atlanta University, my Boaz would soon make himself known. My mother's dream of finding a husband for her daughter was only a few prayers away. In a matter of minutes, I would meet my husband, my life's partner, and the father of my children. There was no way that I could have known that, as my mother desired a good man for her daughter, God was preparing a mature man, cultured and definite in purpose, to receive a wife.

He had finished Morehouse College, one of the most prestigious academic institutions in the nation for African American men, earning a degree in business administration. He was already operating a business at 28 Butler Street, next door to the YMCA in downtown Atlanta. Believing in family-based enterprise, he was in partnership with his brother, Arthur Bronner, Sr.

He recognized the need for a helpmate. A praying man, he did not trust his own judgment but relied upon the leading of the Lord. He wanted to make the right decision, find the right woman, and love her for the rest of his life. Many hours of prayer yielded a rather simplistic response: "If you are looking for a wife and want someone who has finished college, where would you find her?"

In response, he decided to enroll at Atlanta University and take a "fresh air" course while searching for a wife. He quietly but deliberately left his office that June evening to take a course, Audio Visual Aids. Obviously, Nathaniel did not plan to spend his evenings pouring through difficult textbooks. His goal was to find a wife!

There I was in the registration line on campus in southwest Atlanta. Maxine and I had rushed in just before the line closed. There were approximately ten people in the line. I stood there, a little country girl from Forsyth in a green halter knee-length dress (the height of fashion at the time). I looked around and near the front of the line at a registration table was a man who looked at me with a slight gleam in his eye. Gently, he moved and the next thing I knew, he was in line directly behind me. How he got between my sister and me puzzles me to this day.

He stood there, peeped over my shoulder, copied my name from the registration documents, and noted that I was from Forsyth, Georgia. I later found that he was an absolute genius in approaching people and getting to know them. Tapping me on the shoulder, he asked me, "What might be your name and your hometown?" When I replied, he asked if I knew Mrs. Slappey in Forsyth. My yes response then provided the opportunity for him to share that he serviced her beauty salon with professional beauty supplies. He was clever. His conversation skillfully removed any apprehension that I would have speaking with a stranger. He knew someone whom I knew. Certainly that made a difference! After all, the Slappeys were close friends of my family and attended the same A.M.E. church.

By this time, I was at the registration table. He moved near the wall. He waited until I was finished and then ran up to me, caught my hand, and held it. By this time, Mama Maxine snatched me away and said, "Come on, girl, and let that old married man alone!"

It was an embarrassing moment. Remember, Nathaniel was a man of definite purpose. Despite Maxine's obvious scrutiny, he persevered and asked about my lodging during the summer. Before Maxine could open her mouth, I immediately answered, "Bumstead Hall." She might have been my "other Mama," but somehow I did not sense that his character or intentions were sinister. Later, my sister explained that most of the older men were school principals coming to school to take extension courses to maintain certification and to be updated for the sake of their profession. She continued to explain that they flirted with young girls. Having attended the university for two summers, she considered herself a qualified bodyguard, empowered by my mother to protect me.

I listened to what she said and believe me, I found later there were those types of men walking around. But somehow I knew that this man, twenty years older than I, was different. We saw each other the entire summer. We were destined to fall madly in love. I am reminded of a scripture in the book of Ruth,"Blessed be thou of the LORD, my daughter: for thou hast showed more kindness in the latter end than at the beginning, inasmuch as thou followedst not young men, whether poor or rich." (Ruth 3:10 KJV)

Over the course of the summer, Maxine's perception of Nathaniel began to soften. One of her friends, whom she had known for some time, shared that Nathaniel was a successful businessman and highly respected. It was Maxine who broke the news to my mother that I was seeing an older man but a respected businessman. It took Maxine to prepare the way for my mother to accept my future husband.

During the course of the summer Nathaniel and Christine, a classmate of mine, went to my mother's house. Christine was a knockout, an extremely beautiful woman! Marveling at my friend's physical beauty, my mother did not realize immediately that Christine was not the object of Nathaniel's affection. She was absolutely thrilled when she realized that her baby daughter was his date. Her prayers had been answered. Sending me to Atlanta University had accomplished exactly what she wanted.

Nathaniel went to my home to check me out, but instead my mother checked him out. She pulled me to the side and stated comically, "Fool, that man is somebody; stick with him!" Her validation was all I needed and all that she wanted. She then struck up a little tune to herself:

> *Got just what I wanted, got just what I wanted,*
> *Got just what I wanted from the Lord.*
> *Got just what I wanted, got just what I wanted,*
> *Got just what I wanted from the Lord.*
> --Traditional Negro Sacred Song

I left summer school and journeyed to my first teaching assignment in the town of Toomsboro, Georgia, where years earlier my uncle, Dr. Stanley Rutland, had been principal. The Wilkerson County School supervisor, Mrs. Calhoun, made this connection in my interview for the position. Even then, it was to one's advantage to be associated with productive people.

For the first time, I was going out into the real world without Maxine. There were two other young ladies beginning their teaching careers with me. All three of us boarded with Mr. and Mrs. L. C. Curtis, known as

Mama Lizzie and Papa Curtis. They had the largest home owned by Blacks in Toomsboro. It was across from the school and the Holiness church they attended.

Nathaniel's aunt lived in Irwinton, Georgia, approximately six miles from Toomsboro. After a month of settling in and becoming acclimated to my new job and residence, Mama Lizzie called out to us, "Girls, here comes someone. I don't know who, but he's somebody! He is driving a big burgundy Chrysler." We all rushed to peep from the window to see who had come and I instantly blurted out, "That's my husband!" I quickly covered my mouth. I could not believe what I had just said.

My handsome beau walked in, quite humbly and unassuming. He smiled and greeted everybody in the room and then turned to me and gave me a big hug. Wow! It was so wonderful to see him in a totally new setting. I had really started to miss him. That evening we had dinner with Mama Lizzie. Nathaniel knew all of the small surrounding towns because of his business. That night, we went to Dudley's, a restaurant, a funeral home, motel, and barber/beauty shop complex, in Dublin. He knew the family because they were the largest Black business owners in the city. They were well known because of their many enterprises.

It was after our return from the evening that we discussed what we wanted in a spouse. It was a special moment when my Boaz held me and asked, "What are you looking for in a husband?" My mother had prepared me well to articulate a fitting response:

- Firstly, I told him I was looking for someone who had finished college. I knew he had finished Morehouse. ***(Smart cookie)***
- Secondly, I told him I wanted a Christian with integrity and who attended church regularly. ***(Another good and solid response)***
- Thirdly, I wanted someone who did not drink or smoke because I did not engage in either activity. ***(You go, girl!)***
- Fourthly, I wanted lots of children and someone who enjoyed family life. ***(Jackpot!)***

Now it was my time to ask the same question. "What are you looking for in a wife?" I said. Without hesitation, he said that he was looking,

- Firstly, for someone who thought as he thought;
- Secondly, for someone who did as he did and
- Thirdly, for someone who believed as he believed.

I listened carefully as Nathaniel spoke. He had made it crystal clear that he wanted someone (1) who thought as he thought (that's bringing together **one mind**); (2) who did as he did (that's bringing together **one body**) and (3) who believed as he believed (that's bringing together **one spirit**): MIND - BODY - SPIRIT! The key is that God is the connector in the two becoming one (Amos 3:3).

He said that, if he could find that special someone, absolutely nothing within his growing resources would be withheld from her - or from us! Nathaniel had tapped into the success secret of two becoming one.

At that moment, he reached deep into his pocket, pulled out a ring case, and placed an engagement ring on my finger. He kissed me and gave me the wedding ring to keep until that very special day. On that evening, we committed to a lifelong relationship and sealed it with the ring and a kiss.

Looking back, the passion for Mr. Bronner as my husband was already in my heart. The fire probably began to burn that first day on the campus at Atlanta University. I now realized the power of the words in my mouth. I had spoken of him as my husband when Mama Lizzie announced his arrival at her home.

Out of the heart are the issues of life. Out of the abundance of the heart, the mouth speaketh. You shall have whatsoever you say.

The desire of my heart was forced out of my mouth. You shall have whatever you say. So, I spoke it first and then came the manifestation. Always remember, there is enormous power in the spoken word! God simply **spoke** and created the universe. Please note, this was not ordinary speaking. It came up out of my heart. I had absolutely no control;

that was why I put my hand over my mouth. That was the God-force speaking, not me, yet **out** of me.

We were married that summer when I returned home from the school year in Toomsboro. The setting was simple. The wedding was at my parents' home. Nathaniel's mother, sister, my close family members, and the pastor were among a group of witnesses and well-wishers. A wise and frugal man, Nathaniel did not spend **any** money on the wedding. Rather, he invested in building a lasting relationship. He wasn't a conformist and cared less about impressing other people. I can now see his wisdom. He had gotten what he wanted and prayed for and so did my mother. Both desired two hearts blended together in love and put together by God. We honeymooned in beautiful Panama City, Florida.

The Rutland Lineage

Just as there were twelve stones in the Bronner lineage, my family also celebrated a rich spiritual legacy. Nathaniel and I were destined to be connected. The Rutland lineage perfectly compliments the Bronner heritage and dream.

The Rutland family is typified by a long line of religious and civic minded individuals. It has proudly produced ministers, educators – public school teachers, high school principals, and a college president – as well as business leaders, restaurant owners, marketing experts, manufacturers and distributors, and a certified public accountant. The list also includes a medical doctor and a food specialist. Not the least among the descendents has been dedicated homemakers.

The patriarch of the Rutland family was **Rev. Noah Rutland**, born in slavery in Monroe County in Forsyth, Georgia. Noah was a preacher of the Gospel. He married Edna Ogletree.

The **Rev. Elijah Rutland, Sr.**, son of Noah and Edna was born in 1850 in Monroe County, Forsyth, Georgia. He was married to Alice Edge in 1872. He died in 1923 at the age of seventy-three.

Elijah Rutland, Sr., A.M.E. circuit preacher in the 1880s, was cited in the 1973 Forsyth-Monroe County Sesquicentennial Journal as one of the early, outstanding citizens of Monroe County.

Elijah Rutland Sr.

To Elijah and Alice Rutland were born fourteen children: Henry, Nettie, Elijah, Jr., George, Jesse, Hilliard, Wiley, Liza, Gary, Lottie, Lowe, Jim, Alice, and Brinnie. Three of the Rutland brothers became ministers: Elijah, Jr., George, and Hilliard.

Hilliard, who was also a teacher, served as a high school principal in Rockmart, Georgia, for many years. He and his wife, Sarah, had five children: Dewitt, Howard, Georgia, Rebecca, and Susie. Rebecca and Susie became teachers, and Georgia was a dietitian in Pennsylvania. Georgia's son, Anthony, is a medical doctor in Pennsylvania.

Jim became a businessman, acquiring property and successfully operating a restaurant in southwest Atlanta for a number of years. He had one son, W. P., who is the father of a son, Lafayette.

Lottie, like Elijah, made her home in Forsyth. Her offspring included Robert Edward and Wessie. Passing in 1981 at the age of 96, she was the last survivor of the fourteen children. Her daughter, Wessie, is a retired school teacher in Forsyth. She has one daughter, Jessie Pearl.

Elijah, Jr., who became somewhat the patriarch of the family, was for half a century a circuit rider and was admired and respected by all who knew him. **He believed in stability and family solidarity.** Accordingly, he became a property owner early in his career and provided a permanent home for his family even though he moved from location to location as his appointments demanded. He was married to the former Della Smith, who was a devoted Christian and a devoted wife and mother. To the union of Elijah and Della Rutland were born seven children: Fred, Fannie, James, Morris, Alice, Samuel, and Stanley.

Stanley married the former Lavesta Pearson. They had three sons: Stanley Edward II, Kenneth Pearson, and Alfred Wardell. Stanley, Sr., who served in World War II achieving the rank of captain, served as a teacher, high school principal, college professor at Fort Valley State College, and president of Paul Quinn College in Waco, Texas. Stanley Edward is a marketing expert, Kenneth is an accountant, and Alfred Wardell is a certified public accountant and a vice president at the Bank of Oklahoma.

Morris and his wife, Ivester, had two daughters, Maxine and me (Robbie). Maxine, a retired schoolteacher in St. Louis, Missouri, is married to Prentice Foster. They have three daughters: Glenda, Linda, and Gail. All three hold master's degrees and work in corporate America in management. Gail is a retail marketing expert for Bronner Bros. in the Midwestern territory.

I was endowed with religious fervor and married Nathaniel Bronner, Sr. of Bronner Bros. Company, thus uniting two influential families. Nathaniel, Sr. and I had six sons: Nathaniel, Jr., Bernard, Darrow, Dale, Charles, and James Stanley. Dale, Charles, Nathaniel, and James, following the family tradition, have become ministers.

One of the most influential persons in my lineage was my paternal grandfather, Rev. Elijah Jr., and we called him Papa. Della Rutland, his wife, we called Mama.

Remembering Papa

I remember so well and reflect upon the nostalgia of a small Southern town with US 41 going straight through the middle of the community as the main street. Simple houses lined both sides of the road and formed a community of about forty homes. Everyone helped each other and lived in special harmony, except for the incessant gossip and small town chatter indigenous to most rural Southern communities. We played along the sidewalk, on the grass, under the trees, or wherever our youthful imaginations desired to roam. Our fondest memories included our wonderful grandfather, Papa.

We grew up with an unspoken sense of security, living next door to our grandparents. We were sheltered by two sets of grandparents on either side of the house. Elijah and Della Rutland, our fraternal grandparents, were on the right of us; and George and Roxie Moore, our maternal grandparents, were on the left. Our grandfather Elijah stands out as the one who left the greatest number of memories. We called him Papa. He was a proud and productive man who spoke with authority and many years of wisdom.

My grandfather was truly a prophet similar to Elijah, his namesake in the Bible. He was called the old circuit rider. He preached in Monroe, Crawford, and Peach Counties. He owned and operated a forty-acre farm and served in the unofficial capacity as a community banker. People borrowed money from him on Monday and repaid him on Friday—with interest. Learning from others with whom he had done business, he taught us to save. I remember so well hearing him say that "your children don't have respect for you if you don't have any money." We were taught that parents should leave an inheritance for their children. Papa made sure that each one of his sons started off in marriage with a house. He helped build our father's first house, and he even gave Maxine the down payment on her house when she married. The circumstances under which I married did not require financial assistance; however, he saw to it that I was not forsaken.

Early in the mornings in the summer months, Papa would come out with his walking cane and hit the side of our frame house. He would shout, "Get up in there and see God make this world! Rise up early for the early bird catches the worms." He believed in creating one's own job. He was known to boast that he never worked for a White man. Even as a minister of the gospel, he believed in owning his own house and not depending on the church for a parsonage (traditionally provided by the congregation).

Reflecting on the need to be able to think for oneself, he felt that a man was measured "from the neck up." He did not agree with other ministers who said that education was not necessary because God would give you the words to say. Rather, he felt that even though God inspires preachers with words to say, you needed to know the proper way to "spit them out." Having no fear of disapproval, he did not believe in giving the bishop in the A.M.E. church all of his money. This took great courage because sometimes he did not have the required financial report for the Bishop. During these times, he was told to return to his seat and bow his head in shame. In public obedience, he returned to his seat but did not bow his head in shame, knowing he owned his home, took care of his family, put food on the table, and had money in his pocket. He gave as the people gave, and if his congregation did not meet the budget, he was not humiliated by such so-called punishment. He was a man who honored God and used godly wisdom. This taught us that you must think for yourself and weigh the consequences of your actions with practicality and godly priority.

Remembering Mama

Remembering Mama Della Rutland, who took me to Cleveland, Ohio for one month when I was ten years old. This broadened my horizon on a big city, an overnight train ride and a Northern accent instead of a Southern drawl. Maxine looked up to me on my return and was angry with Mama. She was left behind because in those days, we watched Mama milk the cow but we had to churn the milk. (Churning milk is a process of taking the milk after it curdles and churning it until butter appears on top of the milk. Remove the butter and what is left is called buttermilk). Maxine grumbled when it was her time to churn the milk but I never complained. Mama remembered this and rewarded me with the trip. Maxine learned the bitter lesson, it does not pay to grumble nor complain.

I thank God for Papa and Mama. They blessed me more than I will ever be able to share.

My Parents
"Little, in the hands of the faithful, becomes much."

Picture of Ivester and Morris Rutland

As I shared earlier, there are many individuals who helped to pave the way for our family to gain recognition as Christian parents and as highly successful business people. Playing vital roles in this process were both of our parents and extended families.

My father, Morris Rutland, was a classic example of a man dedicated to his home and family. For many years he worked at TRIO Manufacturing Company, a facility where cotton was converted into yarn. He held only one job during his entire working career. He was faithful and went to work everyday. My mother worked as a domestic worker in her early years of employment. Later, she worked in the public school cafeteria as the bread and pastry maker. She stayed on that job until she retired. My parents were married fifty-five years. They were separated only by my father's death.

Though not having the opportunity to acquire a great deal of formal education, my parents remained significant contributors to all that I have learned and accomplished. During extremely challenging economic times, they managed to send Maxine to college in 1948 and me in 1950. My mother was a skilled home executive. She did an astounding job of managing the finances. She expertly manipulated a small budget and used funds wisely. Our household bills were kept current. Every penny mattered, and Mother did a fantastic job of assigning those pennies to the greatest need. Looking back on the whole process, I am sure that she and my father did without as my sister and I gained an education and walked across campus dressed as well as other female students.

I remember once my sister lost our college tuition money. She believed it was stolen while in the restroom. This happened during difficult times. The money had to be replaced immediately. Mother walked to our father's job to share the bitter news. Daddy comforted her and said, "Go on home; I'll bring the money home when I come." My father had a brother, a professor at Fort Valley State College; but he was not the kind of man who begged. He bore his own burdens. Later that afternoon, just as he said, he came home with every dime of the money. My mother sent it to the college—on time! He had borrowed the money from the company where he was employed. He paid it back with honor.

Money was tight, yet we were not poor. We had the things that we needed more so than the things that we wanted. There is a distinct difference. God constantly supplied our needs. He honored the faith of our parents. We saw Him bless the careful stewardship of our mother.

Maxine understood that, being the first to finish college, she would have the responsibility to help me through school before she could marry. There was a two-year period between our graduations. For those two years, a portion of her earnings were earmarked to my educational needs. She married immediately after my graduation from Fort Valley State College. Her financial responsibility to the family ended with her marriage. The day after her wedding, my father took me to the bank to borrow $240 for my graduate school tuition at Atlanta University. It was now my responsibility to become independent and repay the tuition debt.

I think of this often when young people seemingly take for granted the sacrifice of parents who provide an education for them. I wonder how many families today have a similar policy that older siblings will help to provide funds for their younger counterparts. I am forever grateful to Maxine for financial assistance and for helping me to finish college.

My Mother's Parents

My mother, Ivester was born to succeed, March 22, 1909 to the parentage of Charlie and Addie Moore. Both parents died at an early age from heart failure leaving three young children: Bertha Mae, Archie B. and Ivester.

Ivester was reared by her daddy's brother and wife, George and Roxie Moore, who had three girls, Mary, Rosa and Cliffus. Ivester was reared as their natural birth daughter. There was no distinction she recalls, but yet she was old enough to know that she had a natural birth sister and brother named Bertha Mae and Archie B. Oh, how sometimes she longed for them and wondered how they were doing. This was only natural. Archie B. was taken into the Watt's home, but she never knew what happened to Bertha Mae, the oldest sibling. Mother and Archie B. believed Bertha Mae died in the struggles of life, leaving a daughter named Ossie who was reared by Archie B and his wife Viola. Ivester later met and married the love of her life, Morris Rutland, the son of a gospel preacher.

Remembering Ma's Store

My maternal grandparents, George and Roxie Moore, who lived next door to the left of our home, operated a small store that was built beside their home. We (all her grandchildren and great grandchildren) named it 'Ma's Store.' Ma Roxie operated that store with a charge account just like anyone else in business. Little did we recognize that Ma Roxie was charging our little candies, cookies and soda pop to our individual mother's accounts. My mother was lovingly nicknamed "Pig." It was a nickname given to my mother because as a baby she was termed "fat as a little pig." Oooh! That name was attached to my mother all the days of her life.

Ma Roxie was also a distributor of the Atlanta Daily World Newspaper, president of the Baptist Women's Missionary Society, and operated a café in downtown Forsyth. She was an entrepreneur and a mother of the church. Pa was a deacon. They were pillars in the Mount Gilead Baptist Church in Forsyth. They were somebody!

Chapter 2: Our Marriage

Marriage is a spiritual and physical matter. Please allow me to share how our relationship connected to biblical examples and principles. Connections are vitally important.

How do I connect Boaz and our marriage with my own life? My Boaz lived in a duplex at 181 Holderness Street in southwest Atlanta. Dwelling with him in the four-room duplex were his mother Emma and her deceased sister's child Catherine. Times were hard, and Nathaniel's destiny was upon him. With great purpose and tremendous inner drive, you either had to measure up, shut up, or get out of his way in order to survive. He had to make provisions for his family.

His very soft-spoken mother prepared the meals and taught the lesson of how to dwell with a man so filled with high ideals and leadership. She often stated that "a woman could throw away more with a teaspoon than a man can bring in with a shovel." She too was a creative genius. Whatever was left from dinner—whether a sliver of liver, a fork of greens, or a spoon of squash—she frugally put into a container and placed in the refrigerator. Somehow, the next day, it was incorporated into the meal. Remember, this woman was the mother of eleven!

She became a real blessing to me—just as Naomi was to Ruth. And, yes, I knew full well upon coming to Atlanta that she would be a part of our extended household. I knew of Nathaniel's love for his mother and that I should extend an act of kindness on behalf of the man I loved. My husband appreciated this kindness and returned it in more ways than I could ever share in writing.

What if I had said no? I could have certainly refused to stay with not one but two women at the onset of my marriage. I would have missed my Boaz! He was not going to abandon his mother and the child she had elected to rear. It also would have made less sense financially to operate and fund two households.

Mothers-in-law have received such horrible reviews. I am sure that many of these negative evaluations may be correct, but Emma Bronner did not deserve such notoriety. There are plenty of Naomis out there. She was a loving example. This became an incubator for my personal growth, development, and grooming as a wife. God was shaping me to one day become the matriarch of a dynasty, just as Rebecca was groomed to mother Israel. It was here that I learned the importance of looking after your parents. There is a blessing that comes with such effort. I also learned the importance of preserving the ancestral legacy and teaching it to your children and grandchildren. This also comes with a special blessing. I have lived long enough to know that what you do for others you actually do for yourself. We are all connected. It is up to us to establish good connections that are fruitful or bad connections that only birth pain, sadness, and disappointment.

My Boaz initially found me honoring my parents' wishes, living a life of obedience and waiting for my mate. After Nathaniel chose me, he was doubly touched that I loved his mother and was genuinely happy to dwell with her and sit at her feet to glean advice and wisdom. No doubt, there were things that only his mother could help me to understand about her son.

I am old fashioned enough to still believe that good marriages are actually made (ordained) in heaven. History's first matchmaker (Abraham's servant) was dispatched to find a suitable wife for his master's son (Genesis 24). There was one specific command: The woman should come from the far-off area in which Abraham, the father of the son, was reared. The matchmaker set off on his journey and arrived at his destination. Traveling with ten camels, he stopped at the town's well. It was time for the local women to come and draw water. The servant prayed to God for a sign to choose the suitable bride. In his prayer, he asked that the maiden would invite him to lower his jar so that he could have a drink and also offer to draw water for his camels as well—all ten of them!

Almost immediately, Rebecca arrived at the well and filled her jar with water. The matchmaker asked for a drink, and she gladly served him. Then, she offered to draw water for the camels. She completed the act of kindness by inviting the servant to go home to her parents for the night. He agreed.

Before the end of the visit, he had arranged with Rebecca and her family for her marriage to Isaac. She became Israel's second matriarch. The servant saw commendable traits in Rebecca. She appeared healthy, strong, energetic, and hospitable, but the trait that he noticed most was **kindness!** Rebecca had no idea who the man was at first. Her immediate desire was to help relieve him and his animals of thirst and to direct them to comfortable lodging.

So be careful, prayerful, discerning, and not so caught up in the moment. Take time to search for the ultimate trait of kindness. I credit my cousin, James Moore, who has converted to Judaism, for helping me to understand how significant this one element happens to be. I am convinced that this life-changing virtue can change our marriages.

I look also at the example given through the nine fruits of the spirit so celebrated in Christianity:

- Love
- Joy
- Peace
- Longsuffering
- Gentleness
- Goodness
- Faith
- Meekness
- Temperance

All of these components fall under a single umbrella: **kindness!**

Earlier, I referred to my mother as a Proverbs 31 woman. The scriptures describe her vividly with the words,

She openeth her mouth with wisdom and her tongue is the Law of Kindness.   (Proverbs 31: 26)

The Bible says that "It is better to dwell in a corner of the housetop, than with a brawling woman in a wide house." (Prov. 21:9 KJV) Rabbi Milton Steinberg, a renowned Jewish scholar wrote, "When I was young, I admired clever people; now that I am older I admire kind people."

Moving On Up the Road

Nathaniel Hawthorne, Jr. was born while we lived in our first residence on Holderness Street. As Abraham and Sarah moved around according to famines and whatever came upon the land, Nathaniel and I moved around as we progressed financially. When we married, we lived in a duplex. After Nathaniel, Jr. was born we moved to 9 Rockmart Drive. Five years later, there were three sons born in rapid succession. One year apart, we were blessed with Bernard Holmes, Darrow Wendell, and Dale Carnegie. It was at this home we had varied experiences to invade our lives.

Catherine, the adopted sister, married at this location. It was also here, in 1962, that Nathaniel, Sr. suffered a heart attack the very night the two of us returned from Birmingham, Alabama, engaging Jackie Robinson to be the speaker for our annual beauty and trade show (It wasn't international during those days). Jackie Robinson came as the featured attraction the following year, and Mr. Bronner was in recuperation. I became his bedside secretary and worked with his brother, Arthur, to carry on the business. It was from this location that Nathaniel's mother, Emma, went home to be with the Lord.

After Nathaniel's heart attack, I called my mother in Forsyth, Georgia, and asked if she could find some live-in help for our home and the business. She was fortunately able to find James Thomas, who came and attended Morris Brown College during the day and worked in our drug store at night. A cousin, Julia Mae Redding, and my mother's friend's daughter, Shirley Smith, came to help also. When other things beckoned them, they left Atlanta; and Valeria Redding, another cousin, came on the scene.

It was the beginning of a new era in real estate: the great White exodus from the south side of Atlanta. There were homes with plenty of land that became a part of a historical shift for Blacks in Atlanta. In an effort to maintain segregation of communities, a physical wall was constructed to keep blacks out. The barricade was called "The Berlin Wall."

This had to come down. We then left Rockmart Drive and journeyed to this new community. We settled into 465 Fielding Lane. The house was small for our growing family— without a basement but with a lawn that was large and beautiful. It was a secluded neighborhood; the ideal place for four children.

Life kept us on the move. My husband had fully recovered from his heart attack and was back in full swing at work. News broke almost immediately that an adjoining neighborhood was opening and another White exodus was occurring in the community.

It was my husband's custom to take daily walks. On one occasion, he left our home on Fielding Lane and walked toward the Lynhurst area. Here, he turned down Lynn Valley Drive. He noticed a white brick ranch home with a "For Sale" sign. He chose the porch of this empty house for a place to rest. He imagined this same four-columned structure adorned with white antebellum rocking chairs as the perfect place for his family's relaxation. The house was nestled on a hill. The view was perfect.

While resting on the steps, he looked upward and clearly saw the word millionaire written across the sky. He knew that from this house he would become a millionaire!

Thy will be done in Earth, as it is in Heaven.

Earth and Heaven were in agreement.

When he took me to see the house, I immediately said, "This is it!" It was white brick trimmed in pink. I called it my pink and white castle. It had the living space we needed: four bedrooms, two baths, living and dining rooms, den and kitchen, a study, a back covered porch, and a full basement with a two-car garage. We got all this for a mere $32,500.00; but mind you, that was a lot of money in 1966! One month later, we moved into the house.

As we entered into our new home, we wanted to make sure that God's presence and covenant went before us and in us. The Ark of the Covenant symbolizes the very presence of God Himself!

Jesus said, "Behold, I stand at the door and knock: if any man hear my voice, and open the door, I will come in to him." (Revelation 3:20)

The Ark of the Covenant

A Mandate from God

February 26, 2002

Mother,

I was awakened at 4:00 a.m. today with this mandate: "Give your mother this Word from me:

The Lord did not set His love upon you, nor choose you, because you were more in number than any people; for you were the fewest of all people: But because the Lord loved you, and because he would keep the oath which he had sworn unto your fathers, hath the Lord brought you out with a mighty hand, and redeemed you out of the house of bondmen…Know therefore that the Lord thy God, he is God, the faithful God, which keeps covenant and mercy with them that love him and keep his commandments to a thousand generations. (Deut. 7:7-9)

The Ark of the Covenant symbolizes the very presence of God Himself. God's prophets no longer speak from the "judgment seat" but from the "mercy seat" of God. This Ark will serve as a visible reminder that God's presence will never leave your household. It was Israel's most holy relic; now it can serve as that which speaks of God's covenant to you and your seed. I ordered this over a year ago. When it was first shipped, it came broken in pieces with the priests' heads and hands broken off. It came from Jerusalem. The company has since changed ownership, and this time it arrived safely. While it costs about $2,000, its intrinsic spiritual significance is incalculable. May you continue to be blessed and you maintain the covenant of God.

God's servant and your son,
Dale

ARK OF THE COVENANT

Look at the cherubim that sit on top of the Ark of the Covenant; they are facing each other (representing you and your neighbor). They look one to another (toward the Mercy Seat). The wings pointing upward cover the Mercy Seat, and who is there but God. But who do you see? You and your neighbor! Now we can understand God is spirit. **"If a man says, I love God and hateth his brother, he is a liar: for he that loveth not his brother whom he hath seen, how can he love God whom he hath not seen?" (1 John 4:20).** This is what God is showing us with the cherubim. You can't see God, but you can see one another.

What Exactly Is a Covenant?

A **covenant** is a binding and solemn agreement made by two or more individuals, parties, etc., to do or to keep from doing a specified thing.

The Covenant of God

This is the covenant I will make with them after those days, saith the Lord. I will put my laws in their hearts and in their minds will I write them. (Hebrews 10:16)

A new commandment I give unto you, that ye love one another; as I have loved you, that ye also love one another. (John 13:34)

And this is love that we walk after his commandments. (2 John 1:6)

Does not Exodus 25:20-22 explain the Cherubim?

And the cherubims shall stretch forth their wings on high, covering the mercy seat with their wings, and their faces shall look one to another; toward the mercy seat shall the faces of the cherubims be. And thou shalt put the mercy seat above upon the ark; and in the ark thou shalt put the testimony that I shall give thee. And there I will meet with thee, and I will commune with thee from above the mercy seat, from between the two cherubims which are upon the ark of the testimony, of all things which I will give thee in commandment unto the children of Israel.

What's Underneath the Cover of the Ark of the Covenant?

A pot of manna: God fed the Israelites bread from Heaven for forty years in the wilderness. Supernatural provision; the Testimony.

The Ten Commandments

Commandment number five, ***honor thy father and mother:*** that thy days may be long upon the land which the Lord thy God giveth thee. This is the only commandment which has a reward connected to it (visiting them and attending to their needs brings great reward and joy).

I AM THE LORD THY GOD:

1. *Thou shalt have no other gods before me.*
2. *Thou shalt not make unto thee any graven image.*
3. *Thou shalt not take the name of the Lord thy God in vain.*
4. *Remember the Sabbath day and keep it holy.*
5. *Honour thy father and thy mother.*
6. *Thou shalt not kill.*
7. *Thou shalt not commit adultery.*
8. *Thou shalt not steal.*
9. *Thou shalt not bear false witness against thy neighbor.*
10. *Thou shalt not covet thy neighbor's house, thou shalt not covet they neighbor's wife, nor his manservant, nor his maidservant, nor his ox, nor his ass, nor anything that is thy neighbor's.*

These laws (Exodus 20:1-17) to govern our lives are now written in our hearts.

Now with the Ark of the Covenant, we have declared it an heirloom. It will pass from generation to generation as our most holy relic representing the presence of God in our home and in our lives. It's important to remember how God has brought us, blessed us, saved us, and dwelled within us. We, too, have the twelve Bronner stones, the ancestors of the Bronner family, whose legacy of faith we will pass to generations to come, carrying the story of our Lord and our God. This book will speak to the heirs and unto their heirs that the legacy of the Bronners will never leave their households. They, too, will experience God and exclaim, "He, too, is our God!"

Every family needs an heirloom to show and remind the next generation of how God brought them and exclaim that "He too, is our God!"

Rooms in the House

The Front Porch

Twofold Purpose: A Place of Vision and Later Meaningful Retirement

The front porch became Mr. Bronner's favorite spot. He enjoyed the early morning sunrise when he walked barefoot in the morning dew, believing that healing properties were absorbed through the nerve endings under the bottom of the feet. The front porch was where he sat in a rocking chair and reminisced over the roads he had traveled. He mused at some of the old folklore sayings from his home in Kelly, Georgia.

He often told a story about two old men arguing about who had the fastest running automobile. The first one said, "I ain't talking 'bout what the speedometer says. I'm talking 'bout the gwining on down the road," all said while spitting tobacco juice on the ground. Sometimes his telling of the story was so comical that he tickled himself with laughter. He enjoyed talking about growing up and the people in the community.

He sat there and enjoyed his watermelon-eating times. The older grandchildren can tell you how they shared in these times and how he amused them by teaching them how to spit seeds far into the yard across the lawn from his rocking chair. They thought it was hilarious as they watched him in his walking shorts and straw hat, sitting in the chair, propelling seeds for what seemed like an impossible distance.

Now let's take a journey through our house so that you may find the answer to the question as to how we reared six wonderful sons.

Come and visit our Birthing Chamber (our bedroom).

The Birthing Chamber

And the Lord God caused a deep sleep to fall upon Adam, and he slept: and he took one of his ribs, and closed up the flesh instead thereof; And the rib, which the Lord God had taken from man, made he a woman, and brought her unto the man.

And Adam said, "This is now bone of my bones, and flesh of my flesh: she shall be called Woman, because she was taken out of Man.

Therefore shall a man leave his father and his mother, and shall cleave unto his wife: and they shall be one flesh.

And they both were naked, the man and his wife and were not ashamed. (Genesis 2: 21-25)

What a beautiful bedchamber story; and from that standpoint God said, "**Be fruitful and multiply** and replenish the earth." (Gen. 1:28) We believed God and brought forth six wonderful sons and from them twenty-nine wonderful grandchildren.

The Power of the Night: The bedchamber is a place of rest and re-laxation. Be still and be calm. God shuts down the day with night so we can dream, meditate, restore, and sleep; the bedchamber is a place of peace and love. It's a place where we can be fruitful and multiply. It's a place of privacy to shut out negatives. (That's one room that is off-limits). During your private time, take the brakes off. Live, breathe, and have fun. Take time to know God. Give thanks unto God for He is good. Build your altar there or establish a place of prayer before you go out, when you come in, when you lie down, and when you rise up. Be thankful!

What a time for my life to end now?

The doctor announced that my time in this world was rapidly coming to an end. I only had a short while left.

I was happy, I was comfortable, I was just getting to a point where I could really enjoy things, and now this happens!

I have so much stuff that I barely have room to put anything else. My home has become crowded. I truly have been blessed and now I am asked to give all of this up?

I have too much to live for.

I had it all. I was waited on hand and foot. My breakfast was brought to me in bed and even lunch and dinner if I wanted it. I had someone to clean up after me too. I was the most important person around, a real big shot, and now this.

I should have known it was too good to last. I had it too easy. Everything was too perfect. I had no money worries, no job worries, my relationship was perfect. No woman ever loved a man as much as I was loved and now everything is changing.

Why?

Why can't things continue in perfect bliss?
Why can't God leave me alone and leave me happy?
Why do I have to endure pain and suffering?
Why do I have to die?

Why?

Pain is a good indicator that something is happening.
That's why I was at the doctor in the first place.

The pain!

If you heard the screams, you would understand why I was upset. The screams told a story that no medical report could ever say. The screams racked my entire body. I shook all over just from the screaming.

Have you ever yelled to the top of your voice?
Yelled so loud your throat became sore?
Yelled so loud your ears still echoed with your strained and pained voice?
That's what the screaming was like.
I can't even put in words how upset and lost I felt.

Have you ever had anyone describe to you what it's like to leave this world? I don't mean just passing away in your sleep, but to leave in the middle of pain and suffering.

Do you have any idea?

I only had a short while left.

My lungs weren't working very well. They nearly weren't working at all. In these last stages they were filled with fluid. My digestive system wasn't able to process solid foods either. I was on a purely liquid diet fed through a tube. My eyes were very sensitive to light and my house had to be kept rather dark. Suddenly, another scream racked my body.

I only had a short while left.

The doctor's head shook from side to side in answer to pleas for more painkilling drugs.

"We've done all we can for the pain," was the only answer.

I felt my time nearing as I struggled. I am a fighter, but there are some fights that you just can't win. Sometimes what you are fighting against is just too strong.

I struggled anyway.

It was all I could do and I wasn't going without a fight.

I saw blood.

The doctors say this is a sure sign that you have only minutes left.

"So this is it," I thought.
I was too weak to fight it anymore.

I felt myself going down a long dark tunnel.
I saw a great bright white light at the other end.
I felt a strong force pulling me to the other side and a strong force pushing me out of this world.

What or who was waiting on the other end?

Faster than I thought possible; I was pulled through the tunnel.

I knew I had crossed over.

The light was overwhelming, a different kind of light.
Brighter by far than anything I had ever seen.

I looked back and there was a limp body on the bed that I couldn't even recognize. Was this the body that carried me through my old world?

I was in a different world, but was I dreaming, dead, or what?

I saw strange creatures like I had never seen.
They were big giants, but I felt surrounded by love.
Somehow, I knew that these strange creatures meant me no harm.

I heard them speak in a language that I had only heard through muffled dreams.

I heard the words….

Our Marriage   39

"Here is your new son, Mr. Bronner, would you like to cut the umbilical cord?"

This is a MountainWings.com original written by Nathaniel Bronner, Jr.

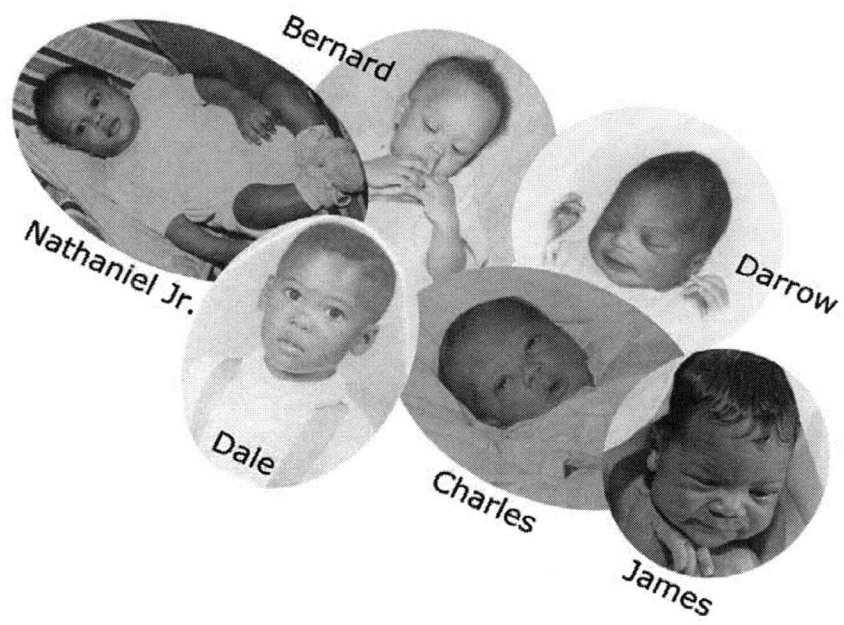

Sons' baby pictures coming through the tunnel

The Bedrooms

I wouldn't dare represent that I speak for anyone but our family. I only offer portions of our journey and how we were directed to respond to God's favor. The establishment of our home and its total operation was God centered. Did we take time to have fun and enjoy ourselves? Sure we did! My husband was a comedian and a clever imitator in his own right during private moments. Many times our days and evenings were filled with laughter that could be heard in the streets. This was an escape mechanism to relieve mental pressure. On the other hand, he was serious and deliberate. He brought significance to every moment, every incident, and every thought. He gave equal devotion to our public moments and our private times.

We honored the institution of marriage and made God the ever-present Father in our relationship. From the very beginning, Nathaniel was very protective of me. He was quite busy and called upon by many individuals for assistance and advice. He saw that the same was happening to me. He believed in balance. He believed that after periods of intense physical or emotional stress that it was important to retreat to rest and rejuvenate. He had seen so many women become unbalanced in religion and neglect their first responsibility: their home and family. God created the family first and commanded us to "be fruitful and multiply."

Looking back on the process, I am reminded of God's balance in the universe. He chose not to leave Adam alone. His life gained balance through the creation of Eve. While Adam slept, God was very much at work creating a being who would help Adam to honor the command to be fruitful, multiply, and replenish the earth. They proceeded to bring forth the first family on earth.

It was very important to my husband that we had rest, relaxation, and a place of escape from the hustle and bustle of our everyday business life. At the end of the day the bedroom became that refuge. The bedroom was a room of heavenly privilege. We were fully entitled to all of its benefits: rest, peace, and love because God ordained it so for a man to love his wife and vice versa.

Included with the expected furnishings of an adjoining bedroom was a place nearby on the floor designated for bended knees. There were also several versions of the Bible, and then there was a telephone whose first use each day was dedicated to connected prayer. There were also many tapes and inspirational books from noted and not so well-known Christian authors and motivators.

There were many times that my husband sensed my weariness or that I might have given too much of myself to those who frequently called upon me to the point that he carried me to my bedroom and closed the door. Everyone knew that I was not to be disturbed. He was always better at declaring self-preservation than I. He would announce in a minute that he wasn't going to let individuals needlessly "drive nails in his coffin." He knew that episodes of repeated aggravation, especially from the same people, were stressful and could produce negative emotions and cause illness.

The bedroom was also that place where we often had quiet and serious discussions about challenges with the business or with our children. It always remained the place where God gave us a special time of resolution and restoration.

Setting the House in Order

Every house needs rules. Every parent should require some sort of order. Our rules were simple, consistent, and carefully explained so that our sons would grow up to be good leaders of their own households. The rules may seem somewhat extreme at some points; however, my husband refused to participate in failure. We did not plan to achieve all of the business successes in the world and then fail at home. Therefore, our sons were expected to adhere to the following house rules:

1. RESPECT AND HONOR PARENTS AND OTHERS.
2. Attend home Bible study on Thursday evenings.
3. Attend worship services on Sunday as a family unit.
4. Attend Sunday school on Sundays.
5. Maintain active participation in the ministry (choir, ushers, deacons, Sunday School teachers).
6. Participate in outlined family chores/household responsibilities.
7. Protection of younger sons by older sons.
8. Employment as newspaper carrier at the Atlanta Daily World.
9. Employment at the family company during the summer months.
10. No dancing. (Further comments below)
11. No drinking.
12. No smoking.
13. No profanity. (Further comments below)
14. College graduation mandatory.
15. No one moved from the house until leaving for marriage.
16. Zippers were to be kept UP!! (Dating began at age 16)
17. Eat to live rather than living to eat!
18. Save your money and give God His portion.
19. Pray every night. Arise with thanksgiving.
20. Think and speak positively (set specific goals and deadlines).

I can just imagine the raised eyebrows and groans as I reveal the list of rules for our home. All I can say is **it worked for our family! If you change the formula, you change the results.**

The Yeses and Nos of Our Parenting

The Bible tells us *to train up a child in the way he should go and when he is old he will not depart from it. (Proverbs 22:6)*

What about when they are old? What about when they are young? The principles and value system are listed later in the book that we taught in the home. I have used room-by-room illustrations to show how and what was the function of each room in the home.

My husband's age was equivalent to a grandfather, thus a lot of wisdom was stored up in him. Having all boys, he knew exactly what his sons might encounter.

- Yes, you teach them the **work ethic**. (Further discussed in the Business section)
- Yes! We all had to work hard. Every child had a newspaper route at six years of age. They were up and out on the routes at 5:30 a.m. carrying the *Atlanta Daily World*. They were required to work in our corner drug store; and as they grew older, they worked in our warehouse and on the beauty salon routes from city to city.
- Yes, you teach them recreationally through sports (golf, karate, judo, swimming, baseball, and football).
- Yes, there are the home chores, school, and schoolwork.
- Yes, my husband used to keep them busy to burn up their energy.
- Yes, being teenagers, the three oldest **(Old Testament kids)** found a way to slip and slide with their extra stored up energy. But the three youngest **(New Testament kids)** beginning with Dale, ushered in obedience and kept themselves undefiled.
- Yes, minimum television viewing. No televisions or video games (No Play Stations, Xbox) in the bedrooms. These are big deterrents in children today.
- Yes, our children were rewarded for good grades in school.
- No! Our children did not stay overnight in other people's homes,

including no pajama parties. You lose control unless you are there with your children.
• No parent went against the other in disciplining the children. This sends a mixed message to the children when the parents are not together.

The Bible teaches **"spare not the rod and spoil the child."** The rod today is our teaching method enforced by the law of the land.

Dancing and Profanity Were Prohibited!

Dancing was a favorite pastime at parties. Parties, in turn, were sometimes connected to drinking, smoking, and excessive peer pressure to do as everyone else did. We felt that it was best to avoid the beginning of the cycle. Even though we had these rules, we also knew that there was a natural tendency on the part of young people to sneak or to "slip and slide" behind their parents back. We never said that our children were perfect. We set rules and our children did not disregard them in our presence. It was set in their conscience. Dancing to the Lord would have been acceptable; however, we did not have this to worry about!

When Bernard became an adult and had his own family, he declared that his children would be normal and purposed in his heart that they could dance if they wanted. He regretted the fact that he could not openly dance as a teen and young adult. When he confronted me with his decision, I simply smiled and said, "It's your time now; do what you see fit. I have done my job as a parent." It was now time for him to do as he thought best for his children. He even put his children on the school bus when he had to walk as a child. James, the youngest son, debated, "Don't knock what our parents did until your children are twenty years old. Then you can speak."

We never held parties in our home. As our sons' destinies began to unfold, I could see why we were under the "no-dancing mandate." At times during our marriage, even Mr. Bronner danced; however, I refrained even though I knew how. God will lead us and guide us if we heed his instructions. **"The steps of a good man are ordered by the Lord." (Psalms 37:23)**

Once again, confession is good for the soul. I vividly remember one day when Nathaniel, Jr. was twelve years old. I returned from an out-of-town trip to a filthy and smelly back porch. (Our children had pets). In a fit of rage, I yelled, "Who put this s_ _ _ on my porch?"

Nathaniel Jr. caught the hem of my dress and tugged it saying, "Don't you ever use that word again." I tried my best to explain my way out, but instantly I knew that God used my child to chastise me. **Conviction is a powerful entity**. As his mother, I never used that word again! I know the word is so common, even my sister used it as a comma, but I could not. It was for the rearing of the children, these ministers.

The Kitchen and the Den

The theme in these rooms became "play and eat." These combined activities changed the flavor of the home tremendously. We had gone from the days of shotgun houses (small homes in which you could stand in the front door and look out the back door) to floor plans designed for family gatherings. Now, the built-in play area converted easily into a study hall at night. This helped to bring together active children, busy moms (who often had to cook), and dads to share common space together. The table became informal as this new space was adopted as the gathering place and the place to eat in the mornings and evenings.

Because my husband and I were both actively involved in the business and the family was so large, it was supremely important that we remained healthy, available, and involved in having fun with our children. Our pine-paneled den provided this haven and retreat. We sat on the floor, slumped on the couch, wrestled with the boys, had great snacks, and made investments in the protection and development of our family.

We reared the children in an era when people customarily boiled greens; beans and cabbage much too long. A sleek man's health-conscious lifestyle discouraged conventional cooking. As far as food preparation was concerned, all I needed to know was how to boil water. The rest was simple. That was good news to a person who had no cooking skills. Nathaniel wanted fresh vegetables boiled or steamed no longer than fifteen minutes. He did not want his vegetables "lying down" from overcooking. Rather, he wanted them "standing up," signaling that they maintained their nutrients and crunchiness.

Did he eat meat? Yes, however, only three times a week (chicken, braised T-bone steak, or beef liver). At the time, he thought this diet was healthy. In later years, he thought differently and made adjustments.

Did he eat dairy? Yes, a three-minute boiled or poached egg and sometimes cheese, sparingly. Through extensive research, he changed his regime after suffering a heart attack (a family history of cardiac problems). He found that red meats were bad on the heart and decided to eat only white meat (turkey or chicken) and fish.

The quest for enhanced health and a better lifestyle led him to Natural Hygiene where he took his family to conventions yearly. Included among the sites were Chicago, California, Florida, and Canada. Our diet then became all raw fruits, vegetables, nuts, and dates. For example, our raw vegetable juice consisted of a carrot-celery-apple blend. Our family had become vegetarian. A good juicing machine and a nut grinder are musts in your kitchen!

As years passed, steamed vegetables were permitted. This program worked well. It required early morning exercise in the fresh air for a minimum of forty-five minutes. It brought positive change in all of our lives. I admit that as a traditional Southern girl, I found myself sneaking back occasionally to good old Southern cuisine when Nathaniel was out of town. However, I knew the benefit of eating right to remain healthy. I had the proof; James came forth.

At almost forty, just after returning from a Natural Hygiene convention, I conceived James, son number six. We called him our Natural Hygiene baby! We had long since discovered that the kitchen was a place where one could either add years to life or shorten it considerably. We chose to add.

Later, I will share some of the other marvelous discoveries that we made in regards to health and the preservation of the body after the death of our third son Darrow. This connection with nature's natural resources followed my family and formed additional business ventures.

Years ago, the dinner table presented the opportunity for families to come together and share the meals of the day. Unfortunately, this appears to be a rapidly disappearing practice. It would be a wonderful thing if families, once again, sat down, had meals together, communicated, and worked together as a unit. It is my prayer that before the family unit, as we know it, completely disappears, we will return to the table.

> **"Give us this day our daily bread."**
> *We thank God for our food, water supply, the sunshine, rain, and clouds.*

The Living and Dining Rooms
(Better named "The Loving Room")

In many homes of affluent families, the living room is a room of rare entry. It almost acquires museum status—look, marvel, admire, but do not touch! This room in our household was a little different. In the words of a younger generation, it saw a lot of action!

First, our sons were allowed to move throughout the entire house. They ran and played and enjoyed everything that it had to offer. They even knocked holes in walls a few times. We felt it was better to have boys who were free to have fun in their home than to have children with warped and underdeveloped personalities. Of course, we liked and could afford fine furniture, custom drapes, and plush carpet; but more importantly than having a showplace, we wanted to build healthy and complete young men. We placed much greater emphasis in building their character than worrying about broken furniture. Consequently, the boys romped and tussled all over the place. We realized that it was important to allow our children to develop at each stage of life…from tricycles, to bicycles, to mini bikes, to trail 70s, to motorcycles, to automobiles, and to destinies that would lead to soaring jet airplanes for ministry. Certain necessary behavioral traits accompany each stage of development. Now, let's get back to this different kind of living and dining room.

We did away with the traditional idea of room structure and converted the comfortable but not lavish living room into a Bible training center. This happened over a period of time. As I mentioned earlier, people came to us frequently for counseling, conferences, or to discuss business matters. We were often on the porch during the day; but during colder months, rainy weather, or late in the evenings, we moved inside.

Even if our agenda was business, we often found ourselves reaching back into our life experience to help others who followed in our footsteps. My husband delivered firm advice in the area of marriage, business, childrearing, nutrition, and health. I held the hand of many weeping mothers and fathers and prayed for their children and for other situations that brought them into our presence. Many times, I invited them to join our family for Bible study on Thursday evenings. Years ago, Bernard, our second son, went to a book fair at his elementary school and came home really excited about a Bible he had purchased. This was the beginning of our family studying the Bible together as a unit. Dale, our fourth son, later became the teacher for the class. God chose him to lead the family into a closer and more involved walk for His purposes. I was really not surprised that he chose this particular child.

God first spoke to Dale at around six years old; and I noticed him around twelve years old next to his bed, praying for what I thought was a lengthy period of time. I continued to do household chores only to find him at that same spot in the same prayer posture much later. I thought to myself, "Even I don't pray that long!" He was in tenth grade when he assumed the role of the family Bible study teacher. By now, the ministerial call was evident upon his life. He had also founded a PTL (Praise the Lord) club at Southwest High School near our home. The first Bible class started in our fireplace room that we outgrew and moved into the living room. Then the neighbors began to come, and later, our employees. The two couches were full and next, the comfortable wing-tipped chairs. We overflowed to the dining room. When it was full, we started to bring chairs from all over the house until we were using aluminum folding chairs!

By now, our sons brought their friends, including their girlfriends. Our neighbors brought members of their families and friends. So did our employees. Soon the gathering had spilled out of the living room, into the dining room, and in the foyer. Finally, the dining room table had to go! We sacrificed having a wonderful and attractive dining area for the purposes of providing a place for God's people to come together and for the unsaved to get to know Him. We left these chairs in place all week because we were busy working people who had all the intentions of continuing to do all God required from us to lead others into the Kingdom.

The piano became an instrument of praise. Dale led us in praise and worship on the piano. He had a magnificent voice. Over the course of the years, many other individuals ministered on the piano as well as in vocal praise.

Our living and dining room became the loving room in the sense that many came to us broken-hearted, discouraged, sick, and confused. The best answer that we could offer any of them was the love of Jesus Christ, and that we did!

Lydia (Acts 16:14-15), a businesswoman, established a church in her house and invited Apostle Paul, who had converted her to Christianity. She said, "If ye have judged me to be faithful to the Lord, come into my house, and abide there." This was the establishment of a church in her house and one of the benefits of Paul's Macedonia call. As it was with Lydia, so it was with us: the **church in our house**. It was here that Dale also performed marriages.

The Basement

This was also the era of "basement frenzy." This terrace level living area provided an additional gathering space and an indoor playground in homes such as ours. It was absolutely en vogue to have such space. The socially elite had big parties and dinners in this coveted space. For us, it was another place for our boys to play and relax and for all of us to have fun. Some families were beginning to install home theatres in these areas as well. We never had a home theatre, probably because watching television and movies was never a priority in the scheme of things around our house.

We did allow our boys to move into the basement sleeping quarters as they became older, usually late in high school or as they began college. It was popular for young men to move out of the home into many of the fashionable apartments available in the city. Most followed a common rite of passage to sow their wild oats and paint the town red, but we were nonconformists. We knew that it only took a moment to get into a world of trouble. Our sons were **required** to stay at home until marriage or, at least, until the marriage was about to occur. We knew we had to make provision by creating a home they would enjoy. We added two bedrooms in the basement and a kitchen just before Nathaniel came home from college. He was pleasantly shocked and wanted to stay home. God had provided a house that accommodated the youngest (upstairs) and the oldest (downstairs). There is an eighteen-year span between our oldest son and the youngest. We worked together with our sons. We knew that we could not just tell our children that they could not move. We had to make the home environment conducive to make them **want to stay**!

When Nathaniel finished college, he was the first son to move downstairs. Later, Bernard joined him and shared the space.

Leaving the Basement: Going to Get Married

Our eldest son came very close to marrying a sweetheart not aligned with his destiny. Nathaniel was ready to move out at twenty-five years old and was engaged to marry. He had purchased a condo from his father that was nestled near a lake. He had his condo and a future wife. Oops! Here it comes. Me and my dreaming!

God had shown me in a dream that Nathaniel's fiancée was not to be his wife. How do you handle this? When I revealed my dream to Nathaniel, he immediately said, "Mother, I had the same feeling and was telling my college friend how I felt just last night!" We knew that we had to bring a stop to the scheduled wedding. How do you stop a well-planned wedding? Where do you start? Who do you tell first? The bride or the parents? A couple of days passed and I heard nothing from my son, so I called my prayer partner, Ann Mitchell, and we prayed. God said for me to keep my mouth shut and not to say another word concerning the wedding. God said he would work it out.

The next couple of days, Bernard talked with Nathaniel concerning the girl he was about to marry. Bernard said, "Man, that girl is not for you. I'll tell you this: I would pay her $2,000 for all her expenses and stop the wedding. It's better to pay her $2,000 now than a million dollars one day after the divorce." God allowed that to really sink into Nathaniel's head. He was servicing a beauty salon route when he told one of his older beauticians he was getting married. Immediately, she posed the question, "What does your mother think about the young lady you are marrying?" Nathaniel stuttered and said, "She doesn't think she's the one." The beautician said, "Son, listen to your mother." The conversation ended with those words.

Coming home from the route, he now had two things to impact him: Bernard's million-dollar warning and the beautician's challenge to listen to his mother. He went to bed that night and woke up at midnight with Bernard's voice ringing over and over, "Million dollars, million dollars, million dollars." It got louder and louder: "Million Dollars! Million Dollars!! MILLION DOLLARS!!!"

Nathaniel came upstairs the next morning and told me his experience of the night before and said he had decided to tell the young lady he was canceling the wedding. All I could say was, "Good!"

Mothers and fathers, I plead to you: Stay on your knees before God for your children. Learn to plead the blood of Jesus over their minds, bodies, and spirits. Also, God had me to memorize the Psalm 91 in two days; I recite it everyday. That psalm is the most powerful scripture of protection in the Book.

Lesson: The Word of God works! Memorize Psalms 91 and speak it everyday.

Chapter 3: The Beauty of Marriage

As our everyday walk of life is revealed, I want to quickly express the beauty of marriage. It is beautiful! From a little girl, you start off playing "playhouse." In the playhouse, you have a bedroom with your dolls that have beautiful hair, ribbons, the doll's clothes, shoes, milk bottle, and diapers—the whole works! As a little girl, you work in that dollhouse everyday. Your imagination becomes sensitive to how your mom and dad treated you. Sometimes, the baby will laugh and you will laugh with your baby. If it cries, you put on a sad face. If it is wet, you make believe you are changing the diaper. Imagining the baby to be hungry, you give it the milk bottle. Sometimes in the process, you talk to the doll just as if she is real and just like your mom talked to you. You talked to the baby doll and held it in your arms and rocked the baby to sleep, then you put the baby to bed, tucking in the covers. Now it was time to go in the kitchen and rattle pots and pans on your stove and take your little tea set dishes and silverware and pretend to eat. In the doll wardrobe will be her wedding outfit, just like you want for yourself someday. You form all of these beautiful images of marriage, and you grow up anticipating living it out to the fullest.

I remembered those childhood memories. Then came the time for me to live it out through marriage. I now had the opportunity to take charge of a real house and find out how different the little girl's imagined perfect experiences compared to life's real experiences. In my little girl's world, I made all the conversations and gave all the advice and had all of the answers. There was no one to dispute decisions; there were no problems, only happiness. This is the beauty of fantasy!

Now, the playhouse was real. I was "unexposed" (the term my husband used) so he could teach me. "In awe" was a pretty good description. My husband was right; I was so kind, smiling and grinning all the time. I was cheerful and submissive, a willing vessel to learn. Nathaniel never wanted to be around anyone with a sad face. It pulled his spirit down. He was sensitive to creative people and those who displayed kindness and cheerfulness. **These attributes breed harmony to the spirit of man from his counterpart.** My husband was cheerful and his creative spirit needed to be attached to that same likeness. Remember, the two are one.

Keeping the Marriage Fresh

Marriage is wonderful! My Boaz went ahead of me and prepared the way. He sent for me to come to the lovely tropical land of Jamaica. Earlier, he found in the hill country a place called Milk River where the hot mineral water flows into both pools inside the hotel where we could wade in the water and relax our tired, weary bodies.

We had fun. We walked in the fresh air as Nathaniel pointed out the acke tree, the plantain fruit, and the banana tree. We enjoyed the papaya, melons, and sugar cane. Jamaica is a land of fruit, sun, water, and fun. Oh, my! Jamaica became the site of Nathaniel, Sr.'s annual February vacation (an entire month) after our Mid Winter International Beauty Show.

It is so important to keep the marriage refreshed by changing scenery. Don't just get in a rut and stay there. Plan to enjoy life; there are new lessons to be learned. It is vitally important that every wife take the time to understand and get to know her husband, research his roots, and along with him discern his destiny.

My husband just loved the state of Florida, and I had a chance to travel there so many times. I became his driver as he used his beige and brown station wagon carrying products to sell along the way. This is how we ate and this is how we slept: selling beauty products in and out of beauty shops.

I remember I was pregnant in 1962 when my Boaz led me to motivational classes at the Dale Carnegie Institute when sessions were being held at the Butler Street YMCA. As we ended an impressive session, "How to Win Friends and Influence People," my Boaz said, "We will name him Dale Carnegie Bronner." Thus, our son received his name during a moment of inspiration by his father.

A Visitation from the Holy Spirit

In traveling the journey of life, it was necessary to die a certain kind of death. I attended a prayer service during which an evangelist spoke into my life. She said that God would visit me within three days. I did not understand the message and had no idea how this would come to pass.

Three days later, I was on my knees praying. My petition before God was that he would "let me die to self to live in Him." I prayed this prayer three times before he moved in a way that I will never forget.

I felt a tremendous surge of powerful energy beaming down into my hands. It felt as though it was so strong that I did not think I could lift my hands. Feeling this tremendous sensation, I asked God to also touch my head and my whole body. The same energy force moved from my hands and went straight to my head, then to my chest cavity, and down to my feet. Wanting all that God would have for me, I appreciated this wonderful and miraculous experience. Just as the evangelist had prophesied, he had visited me on the third day! God allowed me to die to self so that I could live in Him. This dying to self equipped me to become the vessel I needed to become in the will of God.

Mr. Bronner had visited Savannah Beach, Georgia and come home with a dislocated bone in his toe. He was hopping because of the pain and told me he had broken his toe. I proceeded to go and take a shower. Just as I lifted my foot to step into the tub, I hit my toe against the rail and immediately knew I had to go and pray for his toe. Hurriedly, I came from the shower into the bedroom and kneeled at his feet as he sat on the edge of the bed and began praying over his toe. I literally felt the bone jump and move into its rightful place. Mr. Bronner felt it also and was instantly healed. His comment: "Beep (as he nicknamed me), you are somebody!" I immediately brought correction, "Not me, but GOD!"

Marriage: Resolution of Conflict and Anger

Watching the marriage relationship between my parents, I discovered that, if my mom had kept her mouth shut, the arguments would have ceased. My mom knew how to add fuel to the fire instead of water.

Observing these loud episodes, I developed determination not to argue with my husband. Instead, I purposed to keep a silent tongue. I learned later in life that this was one of the most effective tactics that I could have employed.

Nathaniel acknowledged in later years that the silent tongue was worse than a dagger stuck into his heart. It definitely weakened the attack. He could not argue by himself. He looked foolish talking to me as I stared back with no response. It bothered him so badly that he would quickly tell me what I was thinking and then he would respond to what he thought I was thinking. I just continued to remain silent. This left him in an awful predicament. He could not forever continue to talk to himself. Underneath my silent tongue, I was whispering a prayer to God: "Lord, help this man." Through it all, I never said a mumbling word. This became my defense mechanism.

It worked and I knew God had taught me this technique as a child so that, when I married, I would not talk back to my husband. God knew well in advance the nature of the man that I would marry and prepared me to live with him. I used wisdom to determine when to close my mouth because there is a time to speak and then there is a time to keep silent. I admit that a few times, out of human frailty, I missed the mark. One such incident pushed me into the dangerous territory of hatred.

Our company convened regular staff meetings on Tuesday mornings. All of the employees were required to attend. It was during these sessions that we heard departmental reports and received in-service training. We had become involved in selling a product called Slender Now, a weight reduction formula. The product sold for $20 or $25 per can, and the seller made a profit of $5. I saw that the product was consuming too much of our time and was beginning to sideline our own products. When called upon in the meeting to speak, I declared forcefully that our executives were subtlety being enticed by another company to become their sales force. Here we were purchasing their products, providing storage, keeping inventory, and exerting our time and energy. To me, this amounted to a full-time job and an absolute nuisance! I continued to question the fact that this company did not have an established track record. We did not know whether they would uphold the promises made to us and we, in turn, made to our loyal customers.

After my lengthy speech, I could tell that every person in the room agreed with what I said. Goodness! My husband was president of the company and I made remarks that did not support his position. Nathaniel rose from his seat as though he received an electrical charge and proceeded to carry me through the most embarrassing moments of my life. I did not know whether to get up and walk out or just to sit there and cry. I decided to sit there and bear the pain of his words. Amazingly, I kept my head up; but on the inside, I kept asking God to give me words to say in prayer. Knowing my husband, I knew that when he finished this terrible explosion that he was going to, of all things, ask me to pray!

Just as I thought, when he finished, he looked over at me and said, "If you have any religion, I want you to pray." I was horrified and wondered how on earth he could do this to me; nevertheless, I obeyed. I knew this was a test. I loved God and He loved me. He never failed me or left me even in this moment of deep humiliation. Then, I remembered how God did not leave His Son Jesus as he was publicly flogged and hung on a cross. Instead, he placed him there for me.

As I finished praying, there was total silence across the room. No one uttered a word; no one moved. Normally, prayer signaled the end of our meeting. I could tell that everyone, my husband included, felt something. At this time in my life, I was just beginning to study about the Holy Spirit. In retrospect, I know the Holy Spirit spoke through me to warn the company and protect years of hard work and a well-earned reputation. Approximately three months later, the weight loss company went completely out of business.

My husband, like everyone else in the room, had listened to me pray fervently. As I was preparing to go toward the stairs to leave, he rushed to me and extended his hand.

"Don't touch me!" I said with great force. He withdrew his hand, knowing that he was in trouble. I would not speak with him after that. I continued this silent treatment publicly and allowed it to continue for longer than I should have. I avoided his glance and his words and did not want to be in his presence.

Later that same day, he developed cold symptoms and asked me if

I would drive him to Panama City Beach to get some rest. He apologized for his actions earlier that morning and asked my forgiveness. My heart was still wounded from the episode. I did not want any part of hearing his apologies. I wanted to be angry! I decided to drive him to Panama City, but I had no plans to talk with him along the ride. I kept my mouth closed and kept the radio on to break the silence. By the time we arrived at the beach, his cold was getting progressively worse. He rushed to bed with a severe cough.

I immediately left for the supermarket to get medication for a poultice (home remedy pack) made of a face cloth, Vicks® salve, and camphorated oil for his chest. When I returned and had done all I could to try to make him comfortable, he glanced toward me as if to say, "I am sorry." He fondly called me Beep. He did manage to say, "Beep, you are something." He knew that the hand of God was upon me and that I had spoken under divine authority.

The anger did not disappear. In fact, it slowly turned into hatred. It grew day by day. I just could not release it on my own.

Time passed and I had to have a tooth extracted because of this deep rooted hatred. Finally, Nathaniel went on an out-of-town business trip for three days. While he was away, I fell to my knees and asked God, for the first time during this episode, to help me. In response, God told me to read I Corinthians 13 (the Love Chapter). I read it over and over. I had previously memorized the chapter. God said, "Read it again." I did as He said. Then, He said, "Read it again." This went on and on until I had read it five times.

It was then that something seemingly exploded in me. It was the gunshot sound that I heard while giving birth to Bernard. Although I was frightened, at that instant, I was also flooded with love for my husband. A brand new love from the Lord overtook me. I told it everywhere I went. I could hardly wait for Nathaniel to return home. At the perfect moment, he arrived home. I met him at the car. I embraced him and told him what had happened while he was away. He said that he was so happy because he could not have lived with me behaving as I had.

I saw clearly the power of love. It took love to eradicate hate, and the Word of God fixed the entire matter. I overcame by the washing of water by the Word. If you want a powerful cleansing agent, I highly recommend love any day!

Later, I remembered my mother's warning during my first pregnancy. She tried to prepare me for the breaking of the bag of water. She tried her best to give me a proper illustration by saying it would be like the sound of a gunshot. She told me not to panic.

Well, it did not happen with my first baby, but it did happen, just as she said, with my second child's birth. I was in the labor room, staring at the walls, a clock, and the bed. The pain was excruciating. I called for the nurse but could not get her to hear. Eventually, I heard a big blast. It was like a gunshot in the tiny room. Totally forgetting earlier coaching from my mother, I began to scream that someone had shot me! The nurse rushed in and told me that my water had broken and that I was now ready for delivery. They rushed me into the delivery room where Bernard, son number two, burst into the world. This episode connected the natural with the spiritual.

I had to birth love to rid myself of hatred. I had to be born again! This earlier incident with my husband and the growth of hatred was like a natural birth. I heard the same sound in birthing love in the spirit as I heard in birthing Bernard in the natural. Of the six sons, this was the only time that I had that explosive water-breaking experience with sound effects Thanks to Bernard! I still know that there is something different about him. He came into this world with a BANG! I will still have to wait to see his full destiny unfold. Remember, it was announced at his birth: "That's a president," as prophesied by his four-year-old brother, Nathaniel, Jr. Now the resolution of conflict and anger was through love. (I Cor. 13).

When we hear the alarming statistics in regards to divorce, we know that something is wrong in our approach. We should go back and see how God established the marriage relationship and be prayerfully guided with Him as the matchmaker. He certainly guided Nathaniel and me. He will guide you, too. Look for the virtues of kindness and seek God, for He is the matchmaker! He will guide you through all your conflicts and anger. Seek Him.

A Spirit of Jealousy through Vain Imaginations

My husband had several secretaries from time to time. He had such a passion for young, struggling women with children that, if he did not have a job opening, he would create one.

I had been to Panama City Beach for rest. Upon arriving home, to my surprise, he had hired a new secretary. She was a recent divorcee from out of town with two children. They had no place to go, and he moved them into one of our condos that we kept to get away and rest in the city. He did not know how to tell me what he had done. Later, when I met the very attractive young lady, I said to myself, "Okay, I see why he hired her and why he placed her in the condo." Time passed and I was fine with it.

Suddenly one day, we were en route to Atlanta University to hear a speaker from Chicago on the Black family. I was driving. As we neared the corner of Martin Luther King and Ashby St., Mr. Bronner said, "Let me out here. I want to check on some things at the office and I'll come later." At that point, it didn't take much for vain imaginations to overtake me. Yes, that was the beginning point and it grew.

Another day, he was getting ready to leave the house and go to the office. I exploded! He didn't know what had happened to me. He looked around and said to me, "You are jealous." I began the silent treatment with him and that was one thing he could not take. I began to lose weight over this episode as it worked on every fiber of my being. I lost five pounds in one week. He said to me, "Beep, I am going to send you to I.T.C. (Interdenominational Theological Center)." He was old and wise enough to know how to handle the situation.

Here, at I.T.C., having been out of school almost forty years, I had to go back and take a course in Christian Education. How did I even know what course to take at this point in my life? I remembered awaking early one morning and the words came out of my mouth: Christian Education. I began to speak it over and over: Christian Education. It was amazing to me, so I shared it with Dale. He said, "You are to work with children; I thought you knew that." I now had my directives and knew God was in the midst. My idea was to go for one semester to change my mental attitude.

The very first day, we had to buy a journal and begin to write why we had come to take that class. Wow! Did I have a lot to unload. I wrote what had been plaguing me and that began to bring relief. I was not to confront the secretary. This battle was with my husband. The next few days, we had library assignments equipping us to write a research paper. This was a difficult situation. I began to murmur and grumble. Nevertheless, I had to do the research paper and that used all my extra time. God intertwined what I was currently doing—working with children at Wheat St. Baptist Church—with my son Charles working with a group called Disciples to be the focus of my research paper. I got so involved in the paper that I needed a typist. I had to call upon this very same secretary to do my typing. I was so cordial to her she never knew what transpired between Mr. Bronner and me.

Through this work relationship, I discovered she almost hated him because he was so strict about her work. God had to show me in a profound way that I was operating in vain imaginations. That brought great relief within me and set me free. Now, I could understand Psalms 2:1: **"Why do the heathen rage, and the people imagine a vain thing?"**

After completing the paper, the professor of the class called me aside and said he was submitting my paper to compete in the top ten submissions at the school. He was impressed with the paper and said this was a chapter for a book.

This was a prime example of how little foxes can spoil the vine. If my husband had not had godly wisdom to know exactly how to handle me, that nothingness could have ended in divorce over nothing. The situation was not true, yet mentally I declared it true and went through the anguish as though it was true. That is why we should always search out a matter thoroughly before making rash judgment.

In the end, the secretary developed even stronger negative feelings for Mr. Bronner and left the company.

Looking back, how many falsely accused relationships have ended in divorce or over nothingness? You should sit down and count the cost. When you start looking for evidence, that is where your mind and focus will take you. You will find something, and your mind will justify it.

I did not mention prayer; but of course, I prayed. Divine orchestration directed my husband to find a source of distraction until the Holy Spirit could reveal the truth.

Steps to My Release

1. I went to I.T.C. which changed my environment.

2. I purchased a journal and recorded everything in detail that was troubling me.

3. Found something new and meaningful to divert my attention. I had to study. This was a new replacement for my old thoughts. This was my divine movement into my destiny, remember, Christian Education.

4. I had to broaden my views or outlook. I had to visit at least three other church denominations never visited before for service. I visited:

    a. The Jewish Temple
    b. The Lutheran Church
    c. The Catholic Church

    As I expanded my horizon, I was changing myself to see beyond my physical limitations. The God mind coming into focus. I could feel good about my personal development. That is very important stretching the MIND in a positive, productive way.

    Remember the old adage "An idle mind is the devil's workshop." (Give no place to the devil). Do not listen to negative influences from others (remember misery loves company). Keep good company (selective associates) who will help to build you up and not tear you down.

    God will certainly guide you. Remember, He is the Matchmaker! Or should I say He wants to be your Matchmaker!

Family Finances in Tight Times

How did we make it financially with six kids in tight economic times when business was lean? There is an interesting answer as to how we did it.

First, we never tried to live above our means. In other words, we never tried to do or get things just because someone else had them or did them. Our house was simple. We never moved into a house that would cause strain on our budget. Most people, when they buy a house, ask the question, "How large of a loan can I qualify for?" We asked instead, "How much can we **comfortably** afford?"

I will never forget how I first started saving. It was through a Christmas savings account of $10 a month to accumulate extra money for the boys' Christmas toys. In those early days, that was sufficient money. ($10 was a lot more then than now.) I began saving the money for toys, but what happened was I did not use that money on toys. It became my way of saving for the household or for emergencies that might arise.

Interestingly enough, after that first year, I was in full swing of saving. The habit had formed, and it was a delight to save. I transferred the $120 into an interest-bearing savings account and began adding more and more with the joy and thrill of seeing the money grow. Then another interesting episode occurred: every time I reached $5,000, something happened to deplete the account. I did not get angry or frustrated because I was well on my way into saving. I could build it back speedily but kept noticing each time I reached $5,000 that incidents occurred that required the money. It was the exact amount, a $5,000 cap that I could not understand.

Could a divine intervention capture my attention? I knew that something was strange. I was beginning to understand the spirituality of money. God was guiding us by our finances. We were kept so limited that we did not dare buy things we could not afford. There were children to nurture and care for:

- Nathaniel, Jr.(five years older than Bernard) attended Berean

Seventh Day Adventist School for two years and transferred to the public school near our home.
- Bernard, Darrow, and Dale (all one year apart) attended for two years the Berean Church Nursery ($25 a child per week) until time for elementary school.
- Five years later, Charles was born; and when the time came, he was sent to the Catholic school for two years (a cost of $100 a month) and transferred to public school near home.
- James was born five years after Charles and started off in the public school near our home.

I just knew that I was getting ready to save $100 a month after all the kids were in public school. Then something happened and the money shifted. I could not explain nor account for the extra $100 a month that had been targeted for the savings account. The money wasn't there. Something mysteriously happened that I could not explain. It sounds strange but it was true.

This incident led me to seek the spirituality of money. The search led me to the book, *The Richest Man in Babylon by George S. Clason*. I read it and became excited again to discover the 10% formula.

This was great! I had a formula not just for spontaneously saving but with a direct plan that was God centered:

- I had to pay God first, 10%.
- Pay ourselves, 10%
- We had to live on the 80%.

This became a way of life for us. My husband established that he can make the money but I must save the money. That was a beautiful relationship with the two being one. We trusted one another.

This was the first thing my mother told Nathaniel, Sr. concerning me: "Robbie could hold a quarter until it hollers." That was a special key he was looking for, coming from my mother. Money is a serious issue, which is why Jesus mentioned two parables on giving three men money and what they did with it. The first man was given five talents and he doubled his. The second man was given two talents and he doubled his.

The third man was given one talent, and he buried his in the ground where neither he nor anyone else could use it. The decree: Take the one talent and give it to the man with ten talents. Read it (Matthew 25:14-30).

God is concerned about what we do with our money. We were aware of this and tried very hard to live our lives around what we did with God's money.

Nathaniel's uniqueness was he drove an old Buick. He never bought a new car; he did not wear designer clothing or expensive jewelry. He never spent much money on things that quickly depreciated. Rather, he spent his money on wise investments that would restore and build health. He kept his family and families in general seriously on his mind. He didn't have to get caught up in the superficial credit card frenzy of today with overwhelming interest as debt grows bigger and bigger. This taught us budgeting out of necessity. The adage, "Necessity is the mother of invention," was very important to us. The unseen eye, the unseen hand, the unseen mind, and the unseen ear are at work with you in this process. Believe in it! **Faith** is so important when you can't see your way…Faith comes on the scene. Don't neglect it. The words of your **mouth** will pinpoint your faith. Your faith is in GOD.

My husband was a unique soul who believed in God and his principles and could live in the woods or close to nature. He migrated to water and to natural settings. He knew who he was and did not need man to validate him. Humility was his greatest strength. The key is we could have had a much bigger house, but we didn't. His efforts went to developing the business and giving employment to others.

WORK HARD. You must do something to have something.
SAVE. There is something important in that word alone. Think on it!
SPEND TIME. The value portion of your life, with God and family.
OWNERSHIP. Get a grip on your life. Don't rent; **buy** (you figure it out). Think.
PLAN YOUR MONEY AND MONEY YOUR PLAN. (turn around)
KEEP GOOD COMPANY. (selective associates)
BE HONEST. If you want to sleep at night, treat others as you want to be treated.

Our House through Psalm 23
(When Things Seem Difficult)

The Lord is our <u>Shepherd</u>;
He is the One who takes care of us, who guards us, and who leads us.
We must not take things into our own hands.

We shall <u>not want</u>   (Kitchen)
We won't have too little of, be deficient in, or lack because we have to trust God for our provision.

He maketh us to <u>lie down</u> in green pastures   (Bedrooms)
He gives us rest.

He leadeth us beside the still <u>waters</u>.   (Bathroom in your tub)
(Cottonwood Hot mineral pools)
Follow His leading. (Come ye to the waters)

He <u>restoreth</u> our souls   (Living Room)
He gives back whatever is taken away or lost; takes it back to a former or normal condition. It's spiritual replenishing. He refreshes and restores us.

He leadeth us into the <u>paths of Righteousness</u>   (House Rules)
for His name's sake. (The Ten Commandments)

Yea, though we walk through the valley   (Lynn Valley)
(The Lord is the Lily of the Valley)

Of the shadow of death (Transition of Mr. Bronner and Darrow Bronner)
(We learn to abide under the "shadow" of the Almighty)

We will fear no evil; for thou art with us (Ps. 91)   (Never be afraid)

Thy <u>rod</u>
An offshoot or branch of a family or tribe, stock or race.
A staff, scepter, etc. carried as a symbol of office, rank, or power.

Thy staff
A scepter to lean on, royal or imperial authority, symbol or sovereignty

Thy rod and thy staff (Family, ancestors, others and the Holy Spirit)
they comfort me

Thou preparest a table before us (Dining Room)
in the presence of our enemies

Thou anointest our heads with oil (Holy Spirit) (BB hair oils)
(Oil of joy)

Our cups runneth over (our Blessings) (Product vats and tanks)
(Cup of Salvation and the New Testament)

Surely goodness (God's glory) **and mercy** (God's favor)

Shall follow us all the days of our lives

And we will dwell in the HOUSE of the Lord forever.
(Abide with Him)

Our Pointers to Strengthen Your Marriage

1. **Pray**. It is your answer to every problem.

2. **Never let the sun go down on your wrath**. No matter what happens over the course of the day that may offend either party, ask for forgiveness. Reconcile before going to bed.

3. **Always uplift, compliment, and support your spouse in worthy ventures or endeavors**. Become each other's cheerleader.

4. **Keep an open mind and discuss issues**. If you are tired, go out in the fresh air and take a walk. Nathaniel often went to the golf course to release tension and exhaustion. He took whatever was plaguing him and saw it on the golf ball. He then struck it with all of his might.

5. **Study your spouse and discover his likes and dislikes**. I developed an honorary PhD in developing my mind to understand Nathaniel's thought process. That was how I was strengthened to endure his shrewd tongue-lashing. This reduced my times of crying.

6. **Don't forget simple things like "thank you" and "please."** These are power-packed words. They turn your sadness into joy.

7. **Be cheerful and not gloomy looking**.

8. **Remain physically attractive for your spouse**.

9. **Learn to serve each other**. Ask God for a servant's spirit. (Remember the two are one).

10. **Do not agitate or needlessly irritate your spouse**. Remember to be kind to each other.

11. **Keep a silent tongue if you cannot control anger**.

12. **Read Ephesians 5**. (Holy Bible KJV)

13. **Keep a teachable spirit**. I had the best husband in the world. He taught me and I learned.

14. **Take vacations**. You owe it to yourself.

15. **Help somebody other than those in your own household**. (A seed sown to come back in your life) You cannot help someone else without it returning to your own life.

Chapter 4: Boys' Early Years

"How Did You and Mr. Bronner Rear Six Wonderful Sons?"

People always asked us that question. We always wanted children. We realized that children are a gift from God and looked with great anticipation to receiving His gifts. The love and joy that the mother experiences are even transferred to the baby in the womb. Remember the great joy Elizabeth and Mary (biblical cousins) had when they met during their pregnancies. Elizabeth, who was once barren, was six months pregnant when she shared with Mary that she too would have a son. The babies connected in the wombs when the two cousins met in joyful salutation. Elizabeth received the Holy Spirit and began to prophesy to Mary concerning her son. Mary prophesied and praised God for blessing her and making her a blessing to the world. The response of the two babies reacting within their mothers' wombs leads us to know that we must meticulously teach the children from the womb. They hear us and sense our state of mind.

As the baby matures, it soon discovers that your arms and lap provide more comfort than the mattress; and they learn to express the desire to be held rather than sleep in the crib. This is a classic example of the need to train the child and mold his behavior. If the baby is dry, fed, experiencing no pain, and just wants to leave his bed and reach for you, it is necessary at that point to train or you begin to spoil the child. I did both: **trained and spoiled**. Infants often call the directives while young. Parents are just so proud of the first child because there are so many firsts associated with the experience. Afterwards, the actions of the other children coming through the channel are a repeat of what they have witnessed previously.

Most often, they crawl, sit alone, stand without assistance, walk, and then run. More times than not, they form words with the "d" sound first like "Da-Da." The "m" sound is more difficult but comes later for "Ma-Ma." These two expressions cause you to pick up and hold them lovingly. The embrace encourages the child and makes the child feel needed and loved. They begin to walk between nine to twelve months.

Around sixteen months, they begin developing their sentences. The term "terrible twos" warns that they are into everything. A watchful eye, running legs, and outstretched arms are irresistible.

Our first child was placed in our church's day care school. He was still on the bottle. I gave him the bottle before getting onto the bus and after coming home. This lasted about two weeks until I convinced him he was too big for a bottle. Working with my husband about two blocks away, I frequently walked to see him the first week and came back crying. A gentleman stopped me along the way and asked, "Why are you crying?" I explained I had left my baby in day care. The child cried and I cried. These were the days of strong bonding and letting go of my first child was extremely painful. Nathaniel, Jr. was the only child for five years, so he was king of the house and the apple of his father's eye. Nathaniel's mother, Emma, was also a part of our household; so that was another dose of constant love poured out onto him. He reigned as king of my mother's house in Forsyth, too. My husband took note of all this.

When Nathaniel, Jr. turned five years old, his father took him from my mother (who kept him periodically during the summer months) and took him to Tybee Island at Savannah Beach, Georgia. He explained that Nathaniel, Jr. needed development from his father. The next summer he took him to the YMCA and enrolled him in two weeks of camp. One of the weeks, they took the children to Lake Allatoona, just past Marietta, Georgia, to the YMCA Camp. I cried uncontrollably; both Nathaniel and I were not to be consoled. I had to walk away, leaving him in a strange place. I turned around, went to his group leader, and gave him $2 to watch over him. That was a lot of money in 1959.

Beginning with Nathaniel, our only child at the time, it was important to teach the children even beyond the home. We were laying the foundation early for good character, morals, respect, and obedience. They needed to learn how to get along with others, to share, to become independent in growing up with others, to come out of their baby world, and begin to think for themselves away from parents. They had to make their beds, neatly fold and put away their clothes, and learn to keep their environment clean.

These early building blocks were helpful for Nathaniel, Jr., and he got away from the smothering world of a mother and two grandmothers. He entered a world of masculinity. His father saw the need and snatched the child from an environment of comfort to one of great challenge. He assumed full responsibility as a man to train his son to become a man.

Imagine, for a moment, that you are on the scene in our home during the late 1960s. Your father comes to you early one morning and taps you on the shoulder and begins to speak in a cheerful singsong voice, "Good morning! Good morning! How are you feeling this morning?" There was only one accepted response, "Great!" If your answer was anything other than the expected response, then you were in for a long lecture. "Great!" G-R-E-A-T!

"Come, Boop (a nickname given by his father), get up! We're headed off on a short journey. Together, we will explore the community. Don't wake your mother. She is still half asleep." You're half asleep yourself, but you put on your clothes and begin the journey with your father.

The first day of your journey is rather uneventful. You've wandered these streets before during daylight. There's nothing new. A few people are driving off to work and everything else is quiet. The morning sun is just about to reveal itself and everything is peaceful.

Suddenly, in the distance, the train makes its familiar whonk, whonk, whonk sound. As you continue to walk, your father continues to scout the neighborhood. There is a strange yet comforting feeling about this journey, almost as if God is at your side. Your father is noticeably quiet. Something is on his mind. Perhaps he is thinking about his son getting ready to be trained to work and earn a living. Perhaps he's having a flashback of his own early experiences back in the country. It is as though he remembers how he felt as a little lad getting up early to work behind a plow at six years old. As you watch, you know to mind your own business and walk quietly alongside your father. Though sometimes painful, you can be assured he will teach you the right path on this particular journey.

At age six, each of our sons began this same journey as their father prepared them for a life of responsibility and ownership. He purposely made the journey with them. He scouted out the hazardous or dangerous things that might harm them along the way. He made sure that he kept a watchful eye far in the distance. Even though he afforded the privilege for me to remain asleep, as his helpmate, I eventually made the journey with them. Both of us moved together with our sons through the neighborhood. We worked together, making sure that our children were safe.

Sometimes it was raining. Sometimes it was cold. Sometimes it was foggy. The Bronner sons gained the ability to adapt, to prepare, and to be dependable. These were lessons well transferred from Kelly, Georgia, to the paved and well-manicured streets of Atlanta's southwest side.

I understand why Mr. Bronner says it takes a man to rear a man. As a mother, my heart was too tender toward a six-year-old boy going out at 5:30 in the morning on a paper route. It pierced my heart, but I knew it was good for the child. I decided I had to give in and help. The smallest child, Dale, whose route was in our direct neighborhood, serviced forty households. Darrow's route was outside the neighborhood (the next community off Peyton Road, servicing about forty households). Bernard was across Lynhurst Drive to West Manor Lane, a community of about forty houses. Nathaniel, Jr. had a seemingly never-ending route. He took it upon himself and extended the route to several neighborhoods behind Southwest High School. Five years later, Charles began. He took over Dale's route when he became of age, and Dale migrated to the next neighborhood. Then five years later, James began and took over Charles's route. This pushed Charles to the next route, and so the story continued to unfold and expand.

I remember vividly one morning Bernard came to me, holding his head slightly stiff saying, "Mother, I have a crook in my neck." I knew he was trying to get out of going that morning, so I jumped up, wrapped him up, took his bicycle, put it in my car, carried him to the top of the hill, and put him out. It was cold that morning as I took my scarf off and wrapped it around his head. He was able to continue on his route that particular day. I knew his neck was fine, but he did not feel like going that morning. Don't we all know about those days?

Bernard said it was so touching that morning for his mother to remove her scarf and put it on his head and send him on his way. **We never know what touches the heart of a child**. When their dad was out of town, only Bernard tried to tempt me to carry him in the car around his route. Of course, I did a few times because of the big dogs in that area.

We had fun, but it was not easy developing these sons at five and six years old. Nathaniel, Sr. was out every morning, roaming and monitoring the neighborhoods. Our house was located in a valley. The area was called Lynn Valley. A steep, steep hill led us out of the valley in the direction Bernard needed to go. It was a fairly steep incline. We used the incline for our exercises. I went up and down about five times and that was my day's workout. Nevertheless, the route led to their elementary and high schools so the kids had a mountain climbing experience daily. This was indicative of the struggles of life. You need the mountain peek and you need the valley. There are valuable lessons to be learned in both.

As the boys became older, their father carried them downtown to the major bus stops to sell papers and pass out company brochures displaying wigs and cosmetics sold in the three Bronner Brothers retail locations downtown. My husband cleverly trained the next generation to be diligent in another man's business *(The Atlanta Daily World)* while developing all of the skills to carry on that of the family dynasty.

The Teenage Stage

Now, we're dealing with the hormones! How do you handle this stage of life? (See the health and activities for sports section that consumed their energy and see the life's lessons of Bernard and Darrow.) This is the stage where the kids put the parents to the test.

We have to become their living examples. This is the stage where they will tell you:
    We will do as you do.
    If you don't drink nor smoke, we will not drink nor smoke.
    If you don't curse, we will not curse.
    If you don't go out and stay all night, then neither will we go out and stay all night.
    Whatever you want us to be; you had better be the best example.

Bernard actually spoke these words to me when he was sixteen. The veins in his neck popped up as he emphatically articulated these stipulations one after the other. This sent a signal off in my head and a chill to my spine that we were teaching these children by example. They wanted living epistles, not talk. "Oh, God! This is a great responsibility," I exclaimed.

Dale's Walk with God
(as a Teenager)

As we read the Word of God, there comes a time when all of us must be tested. How does God know we really love Him unless He tests our love? Only God knows the heart and will reveal our heart to us. Sometimes, he removes the thing or person that is closest to our heart for a period of time.

From a child, Dale was chosen of God. As he grew, he was the studious one: always quiet, kind, and obedient. Growing up, he lived a very sacrificial life. He was dedicated to God. He heard from God and regularly communicated with Him. He was just special!

I remember once, as a teenager, Dale had to write an essay in school. God gave Dale the words to write. In the essay, he wrote, "When Dr. Martin Luther King, Jr. speaks, he speaks so loud, the deaf can hear him, the blind can see him, and the lame get up and walk." His message was built around the dramatic and powerful episodes in Dr. King's life.

Now, when I think about it, wasn't that the message of the Gospel that Jesus preached? He came to open the eyes of the blind, to open deaf ears, and to cause the lame to walk. The Lord was quietly teaching Dale the same avenue he must travel as a minister of the Gospel. Dale made an A+ on that essay.

He later became president of the student council at Southwest High School and organized the Praise the Lord (PTL) club on campus. This occurred during a challenging time when prayer had just been taken out of the public schools. Dale had Holy Ghost boldness, yet he was a very quiet person. God sent him a strong Holy Ghost-filled lady, Sister

Edna Dillard, a nurse at Southwest High School, who supported him with the PTL club.

I remember him sharing an incident when a bully came over to his desk and snatched his biology folder. Holy Ghost power came upon him and he stared the young man in his eyes with a piercing look and said, "Give it back, in the name of Jesus!" The bully trembled, shook in his presence, and gladly returned the folder. The next day, the young man did not show up for school. Surely he learned his lesson well, not to harass Dale—and the Holy Ghost! Never again did the young man bully Dale.

As his mother, I too learned not to tamper with Dale. One day while we held Bible study in the home and he was the teacher, he said that God had shown him that someone in the class had talked about him. He also revealed that the person was close to him. God said, "I will destroy the person." Dale quickly made intercession for the person. He said God let him hear what the person was saying concerning him like a radio frequency. That put fear in everyone in the class. That night following the class, Charles and James said, "Mother, that was you."

"That was me?" I said.

"Yes," they responded.

At that moment, fear gripped me and I trembled. The next day, I called Dale and asked, "Who was the person who had spoken against you?" He never told me. At that point, he was married and living in his own home. I do not play with God. The very next week at Bible study, as is my nature, I stood up in class and apologized for having spoken anything ill concerning Dale. I asked him for forgiveness before the class, for I did not want the wrath of God to come upon me. As his mother, I had to walk a narrow path with him because he was so special to God. His father learned to respect the special relationship as well.

I remember one day, while at the office on M. L. King, Jr. Drive, somehow my children were there and Nathaniel, Sr. came into my office and was in a rage. This time, Dale stepped between his father and me and said, "Just a minute!" Before Dale could get out another word, his father hurriedly left the room. Smiling, I said to Dale, "I surely wanted to hear what you were going to say to your father next."

Among the children, growing up, his buddy was Darrow. Dale loved Darrow and Darrow loved Dale. Everybody in the house respected Dale. Bernard was the bully in the house, but he never bothered Dale and vice versa. Darrow and Bernard, close in age, were the tough guys. Darrow told Bernard what he wanted him to know and then ran for protection by catching hold of the hem of my dress. Those were fun days!

In the summer months, their cousins Roland and Gerald would come and stay with us. Their mother, Catherine Render, wanted her children exposed to the training of Nathaniel, Sr. Arthur III and Juanita Garmon's children, Richard and Reginald, came and played with the kids as well. Our home was open to other young people who lived with us. Valerie Redding Walters, Harriet Slaughter Pitt, and Carolyn Robinson Mincey were among so many others in this group. I actually counted about twenty people who came and lived with us along the journey. They have all become great achievers in their own right.

Can you imagine Dale in his first car? The other boys' first cars were for themselves; but Dale's first car, an old brown 1971 Monte Carlo, was for picking up members for his Bible class. That was his real joy. He was not dating. He was strictly tuned in to God.

When he was sixteen, I took him to my hometown at Christmas. I took him around to the sick to pray with them. I would stand outside the door, as he would go in to minister. I would sing the familiar praise song "Hallelujah" until he completed his visit. When he came out of the room, I would go in. One lady told me, "Robbie that child is sent straight from God. He told me some things only my mother and I knew." Dale had previously told me God had given him x-ray vision: He could see right through a person. The lady was healed but was told not to go back and do the things she was doing before her illness.

Raphael Green, a young minister from St. Louis, Missouri, brought the message at the home Bible study one night. The message was built in the Scripture, **"Awake thou that sleepest and arise from the dead, and Christ shall give thee light"** (Eph. 5:14). His single message birthed the

Nursing Home and Prison Ministry that emanated from the home. Dale went into the nursing homes and prisons and taught and set free the captives. Many individuals were given directions for their lives. Early on, God gave Dale the gift of knowledge. He spoke to one man and told him he had a good woman who bore his child and for him to go back and marry that lady. The man sobbed greatly and knew God had had to speak that to the young preacher. He had pondered that same thing in his heart. Through a word of knowledge, Dale also told a lady she had a fibroid tumor of the uterus. The lady cried, admitted it was true, and was healed. These were just some specific experiences within his teenage ministry.

Our home was dedicated to God. I took down my dining room table to extend the living room to an area that seated as many as sixty people. Dating as far back as 1977, I prayed continuously and asked God to use us as a family. God honored my prayer and today there are four ordained ministers within our offspring. God had already told Rev. Nathaniel six years ago that Darrow was a minister. God told him to let Darrow start bringing the New Year's Eve messages at the Ark of Salvation Church.

Remember, I said Dale has lived a sacrificial life unto God; and as a mother, I followed him everywhere he went. I knew how Mary felt as she followed her son Jesus. That covers every son but Bernard. Bernard's calling from a newborn babe was president; but as president, he will not be able to escape the greater calling on his life—being a minister of some sort. He already says he is going to reach more souls than all the preachers together because he will get the multitude in the streets.

The Meeting of a Prayer Partner

Dorothy Stokes served as the initiator in another important connection in my life. It was destined to happen and God used her. I invited Dorothy to a home Bible study class that I was attending, and she willingly joined me. She was inspired and told me that there was a special lady she wanted me to meet. This lady was highly spiritual. Her name was Ann Mitchell.

One week later, the special lady came to visit Dorothy, and she brought her to my home. Of course, I was standing in the front yard, totally relaxed, hair standing up on my head, bare feet, and smiling. When the special lady met me, she said in her mind, "Is this who you wanted me to meet? Let's be real now. Could this be the lady?" I guess the special lady was like Samuel when he went to choose Israel's next king and no one passed the test. God spoke and said, "I have chosen none of these." Samuel then asked Jesse if there was another son somewhere. Jesse answered yes and sent for David, who was rowdy looking with his clothes tattered and torn, for he was tending the sheep. He was the one God chose.

When the special lady could not understand why my neighbor wanted her to meet me, God spoke and said, "A barefoot priest." The rest is history. It was not in the outward adorning but in the inner spirit of man. For such as this, a pure heart is what God seeks.

The following Thursday, the special lady came to a Bible class in another community where the room was filled with Word-hungry people in search for God and the Holy Spirit. She and her sister Jimmy Lee Harvey, introduced by Dorothy, both were Holy Ghost filled and tongue talkers. There were others in the class who were also baptized in the Holy Spirit. They began to petition the Holy Ghost for an outpouring of His Spirit so that others in the room, like me, would also speak.

Some in the room began to receive the gift. Most of the energy, though, was directed toward me. I never spoke, although they said I did. Ann looked at me from underneath her glasses with a nod of the head and a smile on her face, as if to say, "I know you haven't spoken."

Another night, my next-door neighbor, came to Bible study and spoke in tongues with the first effort. "My! That was so amazing!" I said within myself. "How could she come in from off the street and speak in tongues so quickly?" Nevertheless, she did and her life has been changed ever since. At the time, she was undergoing a lot of domestic stress. God knew she needed deliverance to handle even bigger things that were ahead. He completely turned her life around and gave her the power to endure.

My neighbor came to my house two weeks later and said, "I want you to see my Bible." I took the Bible, looked at it, and saw nothing different. It was then I looked at her, smiled, and said, "Oh, my God! It is time for us to start a Bible class in my home." I told her to bring her kids, and with my kids, we would have Bible class. The next night they came. We sat in our fireplace room overlooking the backyard. The next week, Sister Edna Dillard, who stood with Dale as he organized the PTL Club at Southwest High, came to the class. The following week a lady came with a group called the King's Kids. We had to move the class to the living room, and Sister Dillard was the teacher. She taught about two months until Nathaniel, Sr. said it was time for Dale to teach. Dale was ready. That was the beginning of Dale's ministry.

Ann became my prayer partner. We began to pray over the phone regularly. That was the beginning of our early morning prayer on Wednesdays and Thursdays at 6:00 a.m. Thirty years represent three decades that God has designated for prayer connection at 6:00 a.m. twice a week. We have been faithful to the call.

It is easy to talk about the good times of laughter together, traveling together in groups for spiritual enrichment, and reading through the Bible at least ten or more years together by phone. Yes, these were the easy going times!

It is not in the easy going times of life but in the times of difficulty that a true friend emerges. There have been two really difficult times to strike my family. First, there was the early morning walk that my husband and I took around the circle in Lynn Valley when half way he began to suffer chest pains. I assisted him to sit and rest under the shade of a tree. Making sure he was comfortable, I ran swiftly to the house to call 911. That was the beginning of a three-month hospital stay where a team of doctors revived him upon entering the emergency room at Southwest Hospital.

Summoning all the children and family, my sister Maxine of St. Louis boarded the first plane to Atlanta as a support system for me. My next call was to my prayer partner Ann. She ran a day care center. Ann prayed first then sobbed. The next thing I knew she was there. After working all day, she cooked our dinner and brought it to the hospital daily. Truly, she became to me a friend as close as a blood sister.

The second difficulty was the sudden transition of my 38-year-old son, Darrow. We faced without warning a divine intervention in our lives. At the home going celebration, Ann collapsed at the casket carrying the burden of a heavy heart before I entered the sanctuary. I was enabled to walk in, view him and not shed a tear. God had sent a burden bearer before me to carry the load. This is the heart of a true friend, a sister, and a prayer partner.

Many people tried to separate us from praying, but God did not allow it. There was another strange episode that happened. Within the same week of my husband's demise, Ann's husband suddenly transitioned. I was secluded in St. Louis with my sister Maxine at the time who was helping me through a period of healing. I had to board the next plane home with my sister Maxine at my side to support me as I went to support my prayer partner, Ann.

Through our prayer times over the years, God revealed through Ann that theft was occurring in our retail stores, even to the point of a description of the person who was stealing. Every time, it was exactly as God revealed through her. This was truly amazing. We validated the details of the description given to us, and the findings led us to the employees who admitted stealing money from our company. God's watchful eye protected us.

How could I finish the book without this story? She was the very first person to tell me I had to write a book over 25 years ago and I laughed. The rest is history.

How God Guided Us in Saving Our Children
(Keep Good Company: Selective Associates)

School was out. One summer evening, my husband and I planned a trip to beautiful Panama City Beach, Florida. We were leaving the children home with a guardian.

There was a young man who wanted to stay overnight with our children. He worked in our warehouse during the summer. We thought it would be all right. That night, after we went to bed, the Lord awakened me. I awoke with clear, distinct knowledge that we could not leave home and leave that young man in the house with the children. I jumped out of bed and told my husband that he had to get that young man out of our house before we left town. I continued, "Don't ask me how I know, but trust me. Do it, for I know God is guiding me. If you don't tell him and get him out, I will." I was so emphatic. He listened to me and said, "I'll get him out."

Well, before getting the young man out of our house, Bernard came to me and said, "Mother, that is not like you to put anyone out of our home."

I answered him, "You are right, my son, but this instance is beyond my understanding. All I ask of you is to trust me as I trust God."

So my husband asked the man to leave our house. About two months later, I had not seen the young man around and I asked Bernard what had happened to him. He answered, "Mother, I saw him in New York at the International Hair Show and he had his hair streaked in every color you could imagine." Oh, my God! Now, you can see why God would not let him spend the night in our home.

God knew what went on in the dark places and saved our children from a spirit that was trying to enter. Oh! I thank God for the Holy Spirit who leads and guides us.

Prophesy Over the Children

Nathaniel, Jr.: A prophet, writer, scientist and minister

>(Discovered at age four and a half when God used him for the announcement upon Bernard)

Bernard: A president

>(At birth, seven days old)

Darrow: A business leader

>(His father spoke over him.)

Dale: (God himself spoke to him at age six so we did not have to validate him.)

Charles: A preacher, evangelist, and prophet

(He prophesied to me and it happened as he said.)

James: An international leader

(God spoke it through Prophet Frederick Collins, Dr. Mary Ellen Strong and Dale was used by God to anoint him.)

Observing the Children

Let's not forget each child has different talents, but from the home, that talent should be discovered. We noticed what the children did in their idle time when it seemed no one was watching. This is what we observed in each of our sons:

Nathaniel, Jr.

Dominant attributes: Bold, truthful, scientific, inquisitive, creative imagination, and kind.

He's an avid reader who read every comic, science fiction, and "how-to-fix-it" book he found. He took apart his first mini bike to see what made it work, then put it back together. During late hours in the night, he worked on his bicycle, go-cart, mini-bike, motorcycle, and yes, later, his first car.

I remember having a conversation with him one day concerning religion. He said, "Mother, you don't have to know the 'how' of things; all you have to know is that it is. You can watch television and never question how the pictures got there. I have to know how the knob brought the pictures into the house through that screen."

I answered, "That's good. I understand and you are right." That was an eye-opener to me and stretched me. I took note and said he would use his head (mind), his hands (body), and heart (spirit) in an unusual way, for he was different. He was a motivational speaker and writer early in life. He could figure things out. I wrote him a letter complimenting him for scientific, spiritual, and business achievements.

I knew he was an animal lover; cats were his favorite. Three Himalayan kittens became his companions. When his maternal grandpapa died, he gave one of his cats to Grandmamma so she would have a companion. She kept the cat and allowed it to sleep at the foot of her bed for about three months then called Nathaniel to come get the cat.

He kept the cats until marriage and would have them today if Puddin' (his wife Simone) wasn't afraid of cats in general.

Nathaniel did not want you to kill bugs. He often said "No, Mother, that little bug won't hurt you. Just pick it up and put it outside."

I said, "No, I am going to smash those bugs (roach, wasp, bumble bee, lady bugs, etc.) with whatever I can find." I panicked at the thought of seeing a rat. I ran and so did all the kids, except Nathaniel and Darrow. They were the animal lovers and were sensitive to God's little creatures. Nathaniel said that they have a purpose and can help you. In comical disagreement, I said, "Yes, they can help me kill myself." We had lots of fun, and each child was different.

"All day, all night - God's Angels watching over me." Mr. Tuffy (Nathaniel) was young and thought he knew it all. He was hot headed and couldn't be told a thing. He was wild with a wild machine: his first real motorcycle and thriller. He was going to test the machine on a city street, opening the barrels up to 87 miles per hour - zoom-zoom-zoom - while having his friend Tyrone on the back enjoying the joy ride. With the speed of a flying eagle, they had to make this curve (God, where are you?). He braced himself to take the curve while he told Tyrone to hold on. You guessed it! He leaned until he couldn't and ended with a great fall. He was frightened! A wrecked motorcycle, clothes shredded to threads, scraped skin, and showing raw flesh - all without a broken bone or having to go to the hospital. He bore the scars and called them beautiful. Tyrone was spared too, but both learned their lessons.

"Angels watching over you all day and all night" took on a different meaning. This was really when Nathaniel experienced God. He has seen God's protective hand over him all his life. God also saved him from the bloopers that Bernard and Darrow experienced during some of their youthful episodes. That's why he can tell you about God and His goodness, grace, and mercy. His daddy's and mamma's God became his God.

Bernard

Dominant attributes: Strong, bold, leadership, sensitive, domineering, competitive, and salesmanship

From a little boy, he always liked expensive toys. One Christmas, Bernard asked for and received a real portable pop up TV/radio. It had a handle on top. While other children were out in the street playing with skates, scooters, bicycles, etc., Bernard was walking around grinning with his TV. He was about six years old. He never broke it but treated it with excellent care. It was kept long after he married until a cousin who had no TV asked to borrow his. He relinquished it to her.

His toys went from the TV, trail 70 bike, a motorcycle that he bought himself, to his first car - a gold Trans Am. Bernard bought many automobiles and sold them to his cousins at a flat rate. He would have paid double and changed cars every two years. Today, his expensive toys translate into Rolex watches, Jaguars, and a Bentley automobile.

He was born to be a president! Follow him further in this role. Remember, they worked from six-years-old onward throwing the Atlanta World Newspaper and as salesmen on the beauty salon routes with our salesmen, covering six southeastern states surrounding Georgia. Bernard saved his money. Bernard was the bully. No one gave him trouble. He wanted to beat up everybody in the house with "I dare you" huffing and puffing. His talent was in publishing and ruling (presidency).

Darrow

Dominant attributes: Leadership, friendly, loving, caring, obedient and humble. A lover of people and animals.

His favorite animal was the dog. He nurtured puppies into big dogs. Later, Darrow had a huge albino dog named Prince. Everybody was afraid of Prince, except Darrow. Prince kept everybody out of our yard but finally had to be fenced in. When Darrow married, he carried Prince with him. Oh, it was so touching! Prince was his friend. Now when you read the letter Darrow wrote to me, you'll know why he took to animals and agreed with the old saying, "A dog is a man's best friend."

Darrow was the middle child, caught between the older and the younger siblings. I remember the Christmas Bernard entreated me for a mini bike all year long. Dale asked for a robot and a trench coat, but Darrow never asked for anything. I found this a little strange. In retrospect, we called on him for everything, and he did it with a smile and with all his might. He could do anything! (I am not including Nathaniel among them now because he was much older). All of this caused me to do something special for Darrow that Christmas.

Nathaniel, Jr. went with me to get the mini bike for Bernard. Instead of buying a mini bike, Nathaniel noted I could get a trail 70 for just $40 more and would have a much better bike. After listening to him, I agreed. In the motorcycle store was a beautifully loaded Q-8-50 bike. When I added all of these fully loaded features, it was only $25 cheaper than Bernard's. It was so pretty and I knew this would light up Darrow's heart because, after all, he never asked for anything and was six years old. At this time, Bernard was seven and Dale was five. Awakening early that Christmas morning, the boys anxiously arose to see what gifts they had received. Bernard grinned from ear to ear. Darrow was overwhelmed and couldn't believe his eyes. His horn blowing, lights blinking, and the windshield guard (like a real policeman's) added that special touch to his bike. Dale had what he had asked for - his robot and trench coat - and was completely happy. I sensed Dale didn't need things for his happiness, even as a child. Dale told me during that Christmas time what Darrow had told him. Darrow said, "I felt like killing myself because I didn't feel loved like the others; but when I saw my bike, boy, I knew mother loved me, too, just like she did Bernard." That was how that middle child felt. Please, parents with more than three children, watch out for the middle child. You never know what they are experiencing.

About a week later that Christmas season, I noted Darrow had parked his bike in the basement. I asked him why he wasn't riding his bike. He answered, "The children are making fun of my bike because Bernard's bike goes faster than mine." (He used the term "blowing mine.") Oh! My God, I couldn't believe that had happened. I learned from that experience: Get them all the same thing, only change the color - maybe yes or maybe no - you had better ask, okay?

Darrow was the athletic child. Everybody thought he was the most handsome of the sons. He wore tailor-made fine suits and the latest fashions; after all, he was the International Beauty Show Director. He loved life and people. Darrow was extremely generous. He was a loving soul. Even the homeless men on the street near his office gathered at his home-going celebration years later and said he never looked down on them. "Darrow was our friend. Darrow never passed by on the other side" was what they had to say about our sensitive and loving son.

Boys' Early Years

This is what he had to say in a letter written to me before he transitioned.

From the Desk of:

Darrow Bronner

Bronner Bros. Co. • 905 Martin Luther King Jr. Dr.
Atlanta, Georgia 30314 • 404/577-4323

Date: 9-30-96

Dear Mother,

As you embark on another great year in your life, I am reminded on how you have touched so many lives, especially mine. Being the third of six great sons I was right there in the middle. I saw the oldest lead and the young follow. Even though I felt that I had to tread different paths you were right there with me. I was too young to be with the oldest two, and too old to be with the youngest three. I had to stand alone. (So I thought) I didn't realize that God and you were there all the time. I do realize your love for me. I thank you for your generous support and your relentless prayers. Mother, I pray that I can be to my children what you and daddy have been to me.

You have been the greatest mother a child can ask for. Thank you for helping me get my house and I pray above all that your years here on earth will be great because you have given so much of yourself to others.

Happy Birthday
God Bless
Love Darrow

Dale

Dominant attributes: Strong, quiet, disciplined, studious, obedient, teacher, complete in God, and leadership

We saw the manifestation of the Holy Spirit through Dale. It was the coming of the Holy Spirit into our home; and we knew it was not Dale, for he spoke in tongues as the Spirit gave him utterance. WOW! This was a tremendous impact on all of his siblings.

He was the child who was peaceful, quiet, liked to laugh at silly things and loved fat people (They were such a delight and appeared so joyous to him.). Dale was my studious child. He didn't play much; you would find him in his room studying. We later found out God was dealing with him at six years old; he would not tell us because he knew we did not understand. He later told me we would have thought he was crazy so he kept it all to himself.

Well, there was that one day that I passed his room and I saw him kneeling at the side of his bed praying. I kept doing my chores and later passed his room again and he was still on his knees. I never said a word but observed the child. I mused to myself, "I can't even pray that long!"

This experience started me to increase my prayer life. I got a clock and timed myself just to see how long I prayed because I knew Dale was praying for over an hour. My first attempt I prayed about three minutes. Oh, my, that was not good. I tried again and it was five minutes. I thought I had prayed at least a half hour. Later, I tried it again and made it to ten minutes. I really thought I had prayed one hour. I gave up and said this child is different. I am the mother and the maximum I could squeeze out was ten minutes in prayer! Oh, my God, this is not good! This was the defining moment in my life that caused me to increase my prayer life. I kept wondering what he was saying to talk to God for one hour.

Charles

Dominant attributes: Quiet, humble, obedient, fun filled, happy, and God-fearing.

Charles was a sweetie pie: quiet, humble, serious, kind spirited, and never gave anyone any trouble. He was a student of Dale's (New Testament child) and six years younger than Dale. He was obedient and did well in school. He taught Sunday school as a young teenager and became a fireball preacher and a developer of young men. He became the teacher and overseer of James, as he was five years older than him. Dale supervised both of his younger brothers, and they followed his example. They experienced the God in Dale that came also upon them. Charles' talent was teaching and preaching.

Operating in the fierceness of John the Baptist, Charles' challenging message "Am I in the Right Place?" was the soul stirring message that caused the Wheat Street Baptist Church congregation to reflect upon whether they were doing what God had called them to do. Nathaniel's chest extended as his son was preaching. That was the pride of a father as he witnessed the hand of God upon Charles as a teenager.

Charles' big thrill was the basketball video games. He challenged all his peers and brothers that he was unbeatable, and they agreed with him. It was amazing! I even believed him myself as he was boasting that he was the world's Number One unbeatable champion. He was persuasive, provocative, and strong willed.

Bragging about his expertise with the game caused James to send out an appeal for a match for Charles on the Internet. James decided to fabricate a challenging response. The response was a computer geek/nerd from California responding to Charles's challenge asking for a match. Charles was so excited. The response read, "I am a computer wizard. If you can beat me, I will make sure you get the national recognition you deserve." That was exactly what Charles wanted to hear. He wanted the world to know he was the video basketball champion of the world.

James heard Charles telephoning his big brother Nathaniel, informing him of the match and that he needed a plane ticket to California. With this level of seriousness, James had to break the news that he had concocted that response and it was a big joke, just a gag. James had created this match to test Charles' ego, but the match was not to occur. Charles replied, "I knew he could not beat me and I knew it had to be a gag!" This proved how much Charles believed in himself; and he continued to brag, "I am the world's champ!"

Boys will be boys!

James

Dominant attributes: Strong, steadfast, high conceptual thinker, obedient, God fearing, and a debater.

I was nearing forty when he was born, and his Dad was nearing sixty. You know he was an old man at birth. He was a special gift for old age parents. His name means "wisdom" and he was born with it. James always liked computers. Early acquaintances and usage led him to develop his talents.

I will never forget the experience when I left Charles and him with my mom for about a month. I missed both of my babies so much but needed the break. The entire family went by my mom's to pick up the two babies and take them to Panama City on our annual family trip. When I reached the yard, Charles saw the car, picked James up, and brought him outside to see us. Charles was five years old and James was about one at the time. I jumped out of that car and grabbed the baby and held him so tightly. I was crying and he was crying; we could not let go of each other. It was a sad sight to see a mother and her baby both crying. After the release, I could then hug Charles.

We packed their clothes and proceeded to Florida. On that trip, all I could hear was the baby's voice saying, "Charles–Charles–Charles–Charles." I felt so badly. I said I would not leave my baby that long again. To this day, James remembers that. It never left his memory. By nature, God has so intertwined or connected us, especially with our mothers. So with the least neglect, the children can register it within their spirit.

Nathaniel, Jr. did me the same way when he was five. I left him with my mom. When I went to see him, he completely ignored me and went to everyone else in the group except me. I cried all the way home because I knew that had to have been God to let the child go to everyone else and refuse his mom.

We have a grave responsibility in caring and developing these children. It takes all of the loving care we can give. It's the little things. So often we focus on big things; but, remember I've said it before, it's the small foxes that spoil the vine. Love is so woven into our fabric of being that we need to give it and receive it. Love is our divine nature.

Chapter 5: Youthful Episodes

YOUTHFUL EPISODES

As you become more aware of the purposes God has for your life, you will realize that purpose transforms mistakes into miracles and disappointments into testimonies.

Bernard's Early Life's Lesson

Early one morning as I came out of prayer, God revealed through the Psalm 91 everything that was happening in Bernard's life. God showed me line upon line and precept upon precept the meaning in his life as it was related in Psalm 91. Even the faces were depicted where words were not understood. Rushing downstairs to his bedroom, laying hands on him, and giving him what God had revealed to me, I immediately began prophesying to him. It was so powerful! I had not done it before, nor have I done it since. It served a special need at that time.

He was seventeen years old and undergoing a challenge in his life. He had become involved with a young lady. She informed him after six months of dating that she was pregnant and he was the father. Bernard came home and informed us of this dilemma. His father was very patient with him, and they had a man-to-man talk.

It was not so with me. I was devastated! My heart was heavy. I could not understand why the young lady withheld the information for six months. I went with Bernard to her home and talked with the girl and her mother. Of course, the mother declared she did not know her daughter was pregnant. I knew this was a cunning situation, and I did not accept it. We left with the understanding that, at the birth of the baby, we would further the discussion. I pondered the situation.

That night I went into deep prayer. I had to seek the mind of God in this situation. That was when the Lord gave me the vision with Psalm 91. Through Psalm 91, Bernard was empowered from the unfolding of it in his life and the prophetic announcement to him. He went in the strength and boldness of that to the girl's home and confronted them concerning another guy she had also dated. His eyes were beginning to become opened.

After the baby was born, there was no resemblance to Bernard. The baby resembled the mother. That left me still puzzled. I had to take it back to the Lord again, and He told me in a dream vividly, "The answer is in the blood and the seed of the righteous shall be delivered" (Proverb 11:21).

I jumped out of bed and rushed to Bernard's bedside. I said, "Wake up! The Lord has just shown me that the answer is in the blood." Bernard believed me. He then told me the three of them had already taken a blood test. "God said the answer is in the blood, Bernard" I retorted! That left an impression upon him.

He went that day to the library and researched the blood. He found there was a test that would provide 99% accuracy, but that test would cost $300. He found the place that offered the test, and they took the blood test. When the test results came, **it revealed that it was impossible for the child to be his**. That had already been established by the regular blood test. He did not need the complex test to reveal it. They did not believe the test results but believed we had it rigged.

If God had not revealed to me in the dream (the answer is in the blood), and **if** Bernard had not followed through with the knowledge, he would have had to assume responsibility for another man's child all of his life. **God is good and His mercy endureth forever!**

Not believing the test results, the parents and daughter took out a paternity warrant against Bernard. The ring of the doorbell at 659 Lynn Valley revealed a sheriff with a warrant for Bernard's arrest. "Lord, have mercy! Lord, have mercy!" was all I could say. Bernard was not home. I called Mr. Bronner at work and gave him the shocking news. He talked with the sheriff, who said his bail would be $1000. My husband with his persuasive soft-spoken voice told the sheriff we would bring him to the jailhouse.

Thank God! I gathered $1000 in cash by the time he reached home. I found Bernard, and the three of us went to the jailhouse. He was fingerprinted, handcuffed, and arrested. Having to look down a long hallway to a jail cell was the longest look of my life, and I could not reach out and touch my son. I know also that was the longest walk of his life.

I did everything but faint! I didn't have time to faint. We had to do something! I can't express what the father felt; I can only tell you about me, his troubled mother. The sheriff ordered the blood test and the results showed that it was impossible for the child to be Bernard's.

Oh, my God, what a day! It seemed like eternity; but in reality, it was about a couple of hours. What if we had had to run around trying to borrow a thousand dollars to bail him out of jail? That would have prolonged his time and intensified his stress. So many families undergo this same experience but, without money, have to leave them there.

DNA tests today are so important and have set a lot of men free. Some even after they have served prison time for several years. However, I thank God for His watchful eyes over His children. Without the vision from God and the words, "the answer is in the blood," my son would have been forced into a lifetime obligation, though innocent.

When we break God's laws as outlined—"Thou shalt not fornicate"; "Keep the bed undefiled until marriage"—there is a penalty and a great price. I salute virgins today who purpose to keep the bed undefiled.

The connection: We need God to lead us and guide us in everyday affairs. He knows every secret thing. He truly led us out of this bleak situation. **"[We] sought the Lord, and he heard [us], and delivered [us] from all [our] fears"** (Psalm 34:4).

Darrow's Early Life's Lesson

God gave revelation to Nathaniel, Jr. as he sat in Dale's Bible study class. God said, "Dale ushered in the New Testament children (Dale, Charles, and James), a sharp contrast to the Old Testament children (Nathaniel, Bernard, and Darrow)." He separated the sons into the Old and

New Testament meaning: The Old Testament children exhibited greater rebellion, and the New Testament children were less influenced.

One of the episodes in Darrow's life created a unique platform to become a better person. From the experience, he gained additional responsibility, compassion, and patience. Darrow learned he would be a father before he had married. This unique episode caused me again to pull from a well of wisdom. His dad stepped in and offered fatherly wisdom. Motherly instinct naturally suggested marriage. It troubled me greatly, but I also knew these things happened when we did things our way.

I prayed, and a strong word came forth to read the story of Ishmael and Hagar. These biblical examples are every day life experiences. God had to tell Abraham what to do (Gen. 21: 12-13). What we send out is what will come back to us. There was no escape. Darrow did not escape it. He had a blended family, and so was Abraham's family. I understand no one is perfect, no, not one. We understand that. How could we forget our teenage years? That is why the statement comes about skeletons in your closets. There was no disputing over whether or not the child was Darrow's, for the child was a beautiful female duplicate of him.

The good news is that God blessed Abraham's seed whether with Hagar or Sarah. Nothing is hidden from God. He sees all and knows all, and what is done in darkness will come to light.

How We Coped When Our Two Oldest Sons Delved Into the Music Industry and Later the Movie Industry

A whole new experience invaded our world as the children started through the positive and negative experiences of life. We gave the children a Christian foundation; and whatever experiences they encountered, we walked with them through it.

I don't know what made Nathaniel and Bernard think they had any professional singing skills. Bernard recognized he didn't have the skills, but you couldn't convince Nathaniel. He became the song artist and writer while Bernard became the promoter. Perceiving big money to be made in the industry, they targeted it. Equipped with selling abilities in the cosmetics world, they assumed those skills could translate into any field, forgetting the talent, gift, and training required for the music and movie industries. (Only Bernard dared to enter the movie industry).

These two brothers had the audacity and unmitigated gall, as their father would say it, to hold an opening night debut. They had produced about ten records, among them "I Am Not That Bad a Man to Love." That is the only title I remember. They had supporters and well-wishers who came to cheer them on as they entered a nightclub in northeast Atlanta. They at least felt like celebrities for a night. They made a poster as the Bronner Brothers.

Baring his chest and wearing black suspenders and trousers, Nathaniel became a musical artist. Bernard had a sleek, sleeveless black-studded, zipped one-piece outfit. They both wore the BB cosmopolitan curl. Bernard knew I would have problems with the poster and came ahead to beg approval from me: "Mother, at least I have my clothes on. Nathaniel has a bare chest." My husband, being the man of wisdom, said to let them go through the experience; but we prayed and walked with them. That was all the control they needed. That made them set some boundaries for themselves, some of which included no smoking and no drinking.

Later, Bernard founded a band and sponsored them on different appearances on weekends. He rented a light blue Cadillac and became the chauffeur for the group. He still has part of this in his system and has lately delved into the movie industry. That sent me into a tizzy again!

All of these were their early dabblings in the entertainment world. Nathaniel said they sold "50,000 copies of their best record and three records went to Billboard's top 100".

Now, let's see how all this translates into destiny and purpose. Early on in the book, I mentioned how Nathaniel, Jr. looked at newborn Bernard and said, "That's a president." He was only four and a half years old. I saw two Ps—a president and a prophet—and I have seen both come into being.

The first album recorded was in a professional studio. The studio cost was so expensive they knew with their business background they could set up their own studio. Nathaniel did it in his home.

The Turning Point: A prophet walked into Nathaniel's home and pronounced a word from God: You will never be successful in this business. All this equipment will be used for God. Nathaniel recorded one more R&B and then turned to Gospel.

Dale's first recording album, "If You Slip, Don't Slide," was written by Nathaniel. Recorded an album for Helping Hands International prayer group, it became the doorway for launching TV ministries for Word of Faith and the Ark of Salvation on TV everyday. Bernard is the associate producer of the movie, *The Gospel,* with Yolanda Adams, Donnie McClurkin, Fred Hammond, etc.

Lesson: Going through teenage episodes? Pray! Let go and let God! Walk with them through it. Keep up with them with a watchful eye. Let them know you are interested in them to help guide them. If what they are going through requires professional help, seek it!

Chapter 6: The Lessons of The Hand

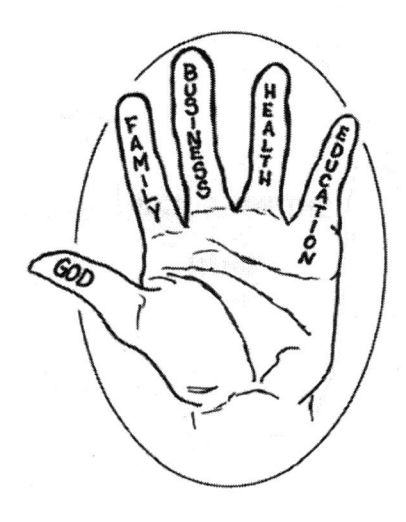

The Lessons of the Hand
The Hand: In His Hand Was His Life's Lessons

Walking by Faith

> **Now the Lord had said unto Abram, Get thee out of thy country, and from thy kindred, and from thy father's house, unto a land that I will shew thee; and I will make of thee a great nation, and I will bless thee, and make thy name great; and thou shalt be a blessing. (Genesis 12:1-2)**

Just as Abraham became the father of many nations because of his faithfulness and obedience to God, God has blessed our family because of our faithfulness and obedience to His Word. Our family has always lived by these basic principles: God first; family, business, health, and education next. We have strong spiritual values in our family, honoring the requirements that God has set for our lives. These are the same spiritual values that we instill in our children, teaching them to revere God and keep His commandments.

God has a purpose for all of our lives, but we must first acknowledge Him by staying aligned to His word. There have been many times that we didn't see the plan and purposes that God had for our lives. Sometimes it seemed as if it was just impossible, but we continued to trust God for His Word and the promises that He has made. We stood on His Word for encouragement.

To keep the promises alive that God has made, we all had to be responsible for our part of the covenant.

The Five Fingers

The five fingers represent the following:

1. **Spiritual Development**: Seeking God first is far more important than the things of the world. **"Seek ye first the kingdom of God, and his righteousness, and all these things shall be added unto you" (Matthew 6:33).**
2. **Family**: No amount of success can compensate for failure at home, according to Mr. J. W. Marriot. A family that prays together, plays together, and eats together, stays together. (Mr. Bronner was a strong advocate of this.)
3. **Business**: **"I must work the works of him that sent me, while it is day; the night cometh, when no man can work" (John 9:4).**

   Occupy until I come (Do business until I come). Be faithful and diligent in business.

   "Seeth thou a man who is diligent in his business? He shall stand before kings" (Proverbs 22:29).

4. **Health**: Early to bed and early to rise maketh a man healthy, wealthy, and wise. (Author unknown)
5. **Education**: This is the most powerful tool for advancement.

These five areas are interwoven throughout the story. These are the life lessons taught by Nathaniel H. Bronner, Sr. to his family and for generations to come.

A Return to the Front Porch for Retirement

In Nathaniel's retiring years, the porch became his office. Instead of going to the office, his secretary came right there to the rocking chairs! He spent many hours on the telephone, closed deals, and dictated letters. He convened scores of conferences and entered high-powered negotiations. Remember, he sat there first. He saw destiny in the sky, and he moved quickly to position himself to receive the blessing.

It was here that he

- Trained Darrow to take his place as Director of the Bronner Brothers International Beauty Show;
- Groomed Bernard on assuming the responsibilities of the president and prepared him to take over;
- Reinforced Nathaniel, Jr.'s efforts and gave advice as to how to keep the manufacturing plants going. During this time he also served as a banker to him in purchasing seven condominiums at an auction;
- Shared with Dale how he was fulfilling his first love with taking care of God's house. That was his underlying mission. He gave Dale the seed money for establishing his first church;
- Sent our sons along their way at the beginning of the day and greeted them in the evenings. It was the place where after he had delivered stern words, that he found an indirect way to say, "I am sorry. Please forgive me."

It wasn't just a porch. It was a godly man's platform to transfer wisdom and a godly spirit and set his children on course for their destinies.

Chapter 7: Sons Seeking Their Brides

SONS SEEKING THEIR BRIDES

And the Bible <u>still</u> says, "He that findeth a wife, finds a good thing."

These stories are presented in the order of my sons' marriages.

DALE'S FAMILY

Dale and Nina

As a teenager, I heard the testimony of a minister who prayed for guidance toward a wife. God answered his prayers and led him into a relationship with a wonderful woman. Hearing this testimony inspired me. I realized that God is no respecter of persons, so I prayed a similar prayer based on St. John 16:13. I knew the Lord knew what was to come as it related to my marriage. So, at 16 years of age, I literally went into my closet with a determination not to come out until God had answered me. After being in my closet on my knees for 15 minutes, I began to get uncomfortable, but I was determined not to stop until I heard from God. After 45 minutes, my back was getting uncomfortable. By one hour and a half, my voice was getting tired, but I was determined to persevere until I received a word from the Lord. After 2 hours, I rocked back and forth, but I kept on praying. Finally after 2 hours 17 minutes and 34 seconds, God gave me a revelation. It was a girl from high school who was 2 years younger than me. In fact, when I saw her for the very first time, she was literally laying at my feet (Another girl had knocked her down.) Since I knew who my wife was to be, I never dated another girl. I had faith and patience. I refused to be distracted by pursuing someone who was not for me. I realized that where there is clarity of vision, there is acceleration toward the known goal. Consequently, at age 22, I married the woman God showed me when I was 16. We have grown in a wonderful marriage of love and maturity ever since.

BERNARD'S FAMILY

Bernard and Sheila

Second Glance

I, a young 15-year-old girl, set out on a journey that would change and impact the rest of my life. On November 14, 1979, I was determined to be a part of Junior Achievement—the world's largest organization dedicated to educating students about entrepreneurship. I was so determined I took two buses to get there. Quiet, shy, and somewhat timid, I entered my assigned room. I slowly filled out all the necessary paperwork. With every opened door, I gave a quick glance at who entered. The door opened again, I gave a quick glance, but this time I had to give a second look. Mesmerized by this guy's good looks, I continued to stare until we made eye contact. Quickly, I looked down, hoping he had not seen me staring.

Someone startled me, saying, "That's the person you give your papers to." After my heart stopped racing and my breathing slowed down almost to normal, I handed him my papers. He gave a slight smile and said, "I will be with you in a moment." Unbeknownst to me at the time, but six years later, this would be the man whom I vowed to spend the rest of my life with. My first date, my first kiss, my first true love and the rest is HIStory.

The Test of Time

The Bible states, "He who finds a good wife finds a good thing." I was in search of a good wife. I wanted to find a woman who was kind, loving, caring, had a sense of humor, good with finances, loved kids, and most of all, we got along very well together. I wanted to find a woman where my goals became her goals, where my dreams became her dreams, and where my vision became Our Destiny. I soon realized I was looking for someone with the same spirit, passion, and heart as my mother. My mother stood by my father through thick and thin. He was a powerful man by himself, but together they became an unstoppable force. I met a woman who had those same characteristics; I met Sheila. I kept her in reserve until we were both ready to make a commitment. Six years later, there was no doubt that she was to be my wife. I found no one else who would stand the test of time.

DARROW'S FAMILY

Darrow and Jane

Before I formed you in the womb I knew you, and before you were born I consecrated you; I have appointed you a prophet to the nations. (Jeremiah 1:5)

God has a plan for every one of us on this earth. Yet sometimes, our own desires and our own will interrupt God's plans. So what do you do when your plan is not lined up with the plan of God? You let His wind blow you in the direction you should have been going in the first place.

God brings to pass what He has predestined from the foundation of the world. What I always thought was a wonderful coincidence I now realize was the will of God in my life. I now know that there are no coincidences—everything happens for a reason and God knows the end from the beginning. I now know that it was God's will that I become Mrs. Darrow Wendell Bronner, Sr. and become part of this great family.

I met Darrow in the spring of 1987 when I was attending Dillard University in New Orleans, Louisiana. I was just going about my business when I was asked by a couple of his salespeople to participate in the traveling road show. I decided to go over to the Hyatt Regency Hotel to check it out. Darrow was the National Sales Director of Bronner Brothers at that time, and he was responsible for the smooth operation of the entire show, including the models. There was all of this activity happening at the hotel, and Darrow was right in the midst of it.

We had been eyeing each other all day, catching slight glimpses of one another as he rushed to and fro directing people. Each time he would look in my direction and smile, I would quickly look away because I didn't want him to think I was checking him out, but I was. I would have to say that our love was not one of "love at first sight." It was one that developed over time, but I do recall how handsome Darrow was to me. He was TDH —Tall, Dark and Handsome. As the day went on, we managed to say hello to each other. Finally during our lunch break, Darrow came over to me and asked, "Can I get you something to eat, young lady?" I accepted his offer and he took off for what I thought would be to bring me a small snack, but that never happened. He was so busy running the show and making sure everything was perfect that I think he forgot all about me.

Later that night after the show was over, I was enjoying dinner with my family at the hotel restaurant and Darrow came over to apologize. "Can I still offer to get you something to eat?" he asked. I smiled and said yes. And after he eloquently asked my mother's permission to take me to dinner and bring me home later, we departed for what turned out to be the best first date I had ever had, talking early into the next morning.

For months after that, we communicated through many phone calls and letters— Darrow back in Atlanta and on the road and me in New Orleans continuing my schooling— and we found that we shared so many experiences. You see, Darrow's and my connection wasn't a Ken and Barbie fairy tale situation. We had each separately become parents as young adults; and having both been raised in a large family within a traditional household, we could easily relate to how our youthful choices had brought such interesting dynamics to our lives. With these and other "coincidences," we found that we could really relate to one another. And that connection grew into a love. It wasn't head over heels, but it was unmistakable.

During one long-distance conversation Darrow asked, "What do you think about coming to Atlanta to finish school?" Of course, I had no idea what he was hinting at, but later I realized he was contemplating marriage. I wasn't even thinking of that. Things had been constant in my life for the most part, and I just wanted to finish school; but God had more in store for us. By then, Darrow had already asked my parents for my hand in marriage. When he finally proposed, he shared that he was tired of running around and wanted to settle down to a life of stability.

The hour has come that the Son of Man should be glorified. Most assuredly, I say to, unless a grain of wheat falls into the ground and dies, it remains alone; but if it dies it produces much grain. (John 12:2.1-24)

Darrow and I met in March of 1987; he proposed in November, and we were married the following June. We married to stay married. We believed that your life's partner should compliment and complete your life, not complicate and confuse it. We both always knew that nothing but death would separate us. We were committed to our marriage from day one—'til death do us part. That was part of our wedding vows, and that is exactly what we experienced: We lived, we loved, and we supported one another until February 6, 2000.

I have come to realize that time is truly a gift that comes threefold. It causes us to reflect back, which is our past. It allows us to look forward for an expected hope and future, all the while cherishing our present. Yes, our present can be looked upon as a gift; that is the gift of today, not yesterday, not tomorrow, but right now—the moment!

You can have all the dreams you want for yourself, but the will of God is the most important thing. For some strange reason, God put me in this family. For some strange reason, He allowed Darrow to have a short life, to have a family, to make a deposit, to plant a seed. God allowed my husband's death to happen. I don't know why. I do know it was the will of God. He knows all and allowed it. Could it be that Darrow had served his purpose and fulfilled what God put him here to do—to bring forth the children for such a time as this?

I have been crucified with Christ; it is no longer I who live, but Christ lives in me and the life which I now live in the flesh I live by faith in the Son of God, who loved me, and gave Himself for me. *(Gal. 2:20 NKJV)*

Darrow's death was a defining moment for me because it meant that the leader was gone and the co-captain had to take the wheel and steer the ship. I had to call on God to give me some direction during that time. The whole world seemed like it was the perfect storm, and I was protected by the Rock. That whole first year after Darrow's death is a blur to me. God really carried me through and allowed me to give out of myself, and now my assignment is to raise our four children alone. But I'm not alone; God is with me, but I miss Darrow. He was such a nurturing man. He had finesse. He was always giving a helping hand, always pointing people in the right direction; and he always took things to the next level; he never left things the same, including me.

In the years since Darrow died, I have been stretched to my limits, grown so much and learned more than I ever thought possible. I've learned that it's okay to be single and whole all the way around—spiritually, emotionally, physically, and financially. I've learned that it's okay to be you, but you don't really know who you are until you get a revelation of who God is. You can do a lot for God if you just wait for Him to show you His will.

Darrow was a gift that God gave to me; it was in His will. I didn't find Darrow; he found me. I don't know if it's God's will that I marry again, but I know what it was to love Darrow Bronner. Because of what we had together, I've set standards and expectations for myself and for our children. And because of the awesome man he was, there's no way I could even compare anyone to him.

CHARLES' FAMILY

Charles and Traci

I met my wife (Traci) in 1984 at Wheat Street Baptist Church. I was sixteen years old, and I had finally attained the required minimum age to begin dating. My parents had a rule that their sons couldn't begin dating until the age of sixteen. Now, having not only a driver's license but a dating license as well, I eagerly looked forward to my first date.

While attending church on Sundays, I began to pay very close attention to the Scripture reciting portion of the service. Not that I was so interested in Scripture, but there was a tall, slim, beautiful young lady with long, black hair flowing down her back, reciting the most beautiful verses I have ever heard. It was love at first sight! From that point on, going to church was the new highlight of my week.

I could hardly wait for Sundays to come because I knew I would see the young lady who caused butterflies in my stomach. For weeks, I watched her and dreamt about her; but I had only one problem: I was too shy to introduce myself. After much consideration, I decided I must get someone to introduce us. Sure enough, I did! We finally met; neither of us said very much, but that began the spark to a beautiful relationship. We dated throughout high school and college for a total of six years. We both knew we were destined to be together forever; and in 1991 I asked Traci Michelle Jenkins to be my wife.

NATHANIEL'S FAMILY

Nathaniel and Stacey

(How I Met Puddin)

I had a saying in college concerning romance. The college years were rather free, but the principles remained the same even for life after college. I saw romances in college blossom then wither. I see the same thing now. My saying was this: You had to find them, you had to get them, and you had to keep them. It's the essence of courtship and marriage.

I was 27 when I met my wife. I remember when I first saw her. She had on a pair of white, tight fitting pants. I was visiting friends in St. Petersburg, Florida, where I had graduated from Eckerd College. Several of us had gotten together for old times' sake since it had been six years since graduation. One of those friends was Peter Rowe. Pete or, as we called him, "The Doctor" was my college roommate for my first three years of college. I'm not sure where he got the nickname The Doctor.

Perhaps it was because with his glasses and matter-of-fact demeanor, he reminded people of a doctor.

The Doctor came from his home in Clearwater, Florida, to meet me in St. Petersburg. The Doctor was not alone. He brought with him his niece, Stacey. Stacey didn't normally follow her uncle around. As a matter of fact, I don't think Stacey went anywhere with her uncle. So what was she doing with The Doctor in St. Petersburg?

I was in the music business. My brother Bernard and I formed the Bronner Brothers singing group. We made R&B music, or rather I made the music and Bernard did the promoting. We had three songs that made it to Billboard's top 100. At our musical peak, we had billboards, magazine articles and ads, radio play, and posters.

Inside of every album (In that day, CDs weren't around, only cassettes and albums) was a poster. On the poster was a picture of Bernard and me. Bernard had on a black jacket. I had on black suspenders. What was under the black suspenders? Me. I didn't have on a shirt. That poster was on Stacey's bedroom wall; thus her trip with Uncle Peter, The Doctor, to see his college roommate, the man on her bedroom wall.

I was 27. She was 16.

I remember the white pants, and I remember her saying when she saw me, "You look bigger on the poster." After a few minutes during that night with Uncle Peter and Stacey, I didn't see her again for ten years. What happened before and during those ten years is enough to fill a book by itself. As a matter of fact, it is a book; I've written it, but I haven't published it and probably never will.

Ten years after the meeting in St. Petersburg, The Doctor called me. "Do you remember my niece Stacey?" he asked.

"Yes," I truthfully answered. I believe there was also someone else with The Doctor that night but I can't remember them. I only remembered Stacey, the white pants, the animated little girl with the frank and unflattering comments.

"She's coming to Atlanta for a training seminar with UPS and she wanted me to ask you if you would show her around Atlanta," The Doctor said.

"Sure," I answered. After all, I had shared a room with The Doctor for three years in peace. I would gladly do it.

I talked with Stacey on the phone and got the location where she was. She talked fast. She was still animated. She wasn't exactly my kind of woman since I consider myself more the quiet introspective type. Anyway, I had promised The Doctor.

Stacey was to be in Atlanta at the training seminar for about a week. I picked her up at the hotel where she was staying. She was now a very pretty young woman of 26. I was 37. I took her to my favorite restaurant, Veggieland. Veggieland was a vegetarian restaurant. She didn't like it and didn't eat anything. Our next meal was at Shoney's where she could get food more suitable to her palate.

We were as different as our food desires. I knew the differences: They stood out like oil stands on water, but yet we talked a considerable amount. Stacey was still very animated and when she talked she used her hands. She had a habit of touching me as she talked. She didn't touch my skin, just my shirt.

That's when it got weird.

When she touched me, even just the shirt, it sent literal electric energy through me. It happened on the first day that she touched me. That had never happened with any other woman. After about three days I just said, "Stop touching me!"

"Why?" she inquired.

"Because it's sending something through me that I can't explain," was something like my answer.

My search for a wife had been a long and complicated one. It was what I would call in mild terms an adventure. It was the search and corresponding experiences that made my spiritual belief stronger.

Stacey was also different in another aspect. She was 26 (27 by the time that we married) and she was STILL a virgin. She didn't just tell me beforehand; I know it was an absolute fact from the wedding night.

A few months after Stacey came to Atlanta for the week of training, the church that I now pastor, The ARK of Salvation had begun. My younger brother, C. Elijah, was the pastor for the first five years. C. Elijah had been ordained and preaching for a long time. I had done neither, although I had been keynote speaker at several events. I had the prophecies of my preaching and being a pastor long before I accepted it, either in actual deed or in mental acceptance.

When the church became available and C. Elijah was offered the pastorship, he said that he would be the pastor only on one condition: that his elder brother Nathaniel is the co-pastor. I was directly hearing from God at the time and He spoke to me, "You cannot enter the pulpit as a single man." That was two months before the church was to open.

On Friday, September 23, 1994, I was ordained.
On Saturday September 24, 1994, I was married to Stacey.
On Sunday September 25, 1994, I began as co-pastor of The ARK of Salvation.

The two-month span between hearing the voice of God saying that I could not enter the pulpit as a single man and the resulting walking down the aisle is yet another saga.

I now call Stacey "Puddin." She is the mother of our four boys: Nathaniel III, Josees, Christian, and George. Puddin and I still have animated discussions about the other two boys God has spoken who are destined to come, the next being Josiah.

I have absolutely no doubt whatsoever that Puddin was destined to be in my life and my wife. I am and have always been an adventurer. It's been, and continues to be, an adventure.

JAMES' FAMILY

James and Stephanie

(My Search for a Wife)

My thoughts of finding a wife came very early in life. I was a fortunate young man whose role models slept in the same room with him, ate at the same table, and shared the same parents. By the example of my two brothers closest to me in age and a heart desirous of pleasing God at all costs, I made a vow unto God at the age of 15 to keep the bed undefiled until marriage. I prayed and told God that I would keep my bodily temple dedicated unto him, and in return I asked him to guide me to the wife that he desired for me. I knew even at the age of 15 that the choice of a mate would be the most impacting decision of my entire life, second only to my choice of spiritual path. I knew that people made decisions to marry everyday based on what they were feeling, but most marriages didn't last.

Knowing myself and the vow that I had made to God, I knew I needed to marry at a fairly young age because life is filled with constant temptations. I set a goal of finding my wife by the time I finished college. Having the Bronner name, I knew that many women would be attracted to who I was and what I could offer them more so than wanting me for me. Before praying for the woman that I would spend the rest of my life with, I sat down and thought exactly what it was that I was looking for and how specifically to word my request for it. The first thing you notice about women is beauty; but then I thought, even though beauty is exciting, prideful, and hormonally stimulating, I knew many men who had stunning women but were not happy with them. My mind next went to intelligence and talent. It would be nice to marry someone smart and gifted to pass these traits to the children and to help accomplish great things in life. Then I thought about many girls whom I knew who were beautiful, smart, and gifted, yet they had an air that exuded vanity or arrogance.

Finally, I thought to myself, "My mother is the highest quality woman that I know and have ever met; what is it that she has that is rare?" Even though my mother was beautiful, smart, and talented, I knew that neither of these were her greatest and most precious quality. The answer to my meditation on the question was, "My mother has a heart of gold." My mother's heart cry in life was, "I desire to please God." Everything that she did embodied that desire. She knew that to please God she must raise her children in the knowledge of him. She knew to please God she must submit unto the God given authority of her husband and encourage and support him when life would want to tear him down. Many mornings I was awakened to the sound of her praying, strengthening her connection to God so that she would know his will in order to perform it. Out of prayer, she was told that she must learn Scripture; from Scripture she learned that she must disciple more than just her family. I saw her drive her Mercedes into crime-ridden, poverty areas of the city and knock on the doors of those who sold drugs and sell them into releasing their children unto her care for spiritual training. I saw her bow her pride many a time whenever she had said anything to hurt someone; she would confess what she had done in front of groups and ask not only for God's forgiveness but the more difficult forgiveness of the person. I knew that what made my mother the virtuous woman that the book of Proverbs only partially described was her heart of gold.

At this point of enlightenment, all of my humanly desire melted away and I took pen and paper and wrote the following request to God: "Lord, send me a wife with the heart of my mother." I took this paper and slept with it under my mattress for seven years until my prayer was answered. It was at a Bronner Bros. Mid-Summer Beauty Show that God began to tap me on the shoulder and say here she is. Sitting here at the computer writing this page for my mother's book, God just showed me for the first time the revelation of one of the hints he was giving me at the time. Out of hundreds of booths at the convention center, God placed my wife at a particular booth and hung a sign over the booth that was meant just for me. In my senior year in college, at a time in my life where I told the Lord, "I am ready to get married now, Lord; who am I to marry," her booth read, "Ask Me."

I saw a girl sitting at a booth. I already knew her because she graduated a year ahead of me from my high school. My mind told me that she is older than I am by a year and would not be interested in me, but something seemed so special about her. I was too bashful to say more than a friendly "Hello, how have you been?" But when I got back to my booth, boy, did I begin to talk! I told everyone who would listen how beautiful and sweet the girl was at the booth out front. My sister-in-law decided she would do something about it; so without my permission and definitely without my knowledge, she went out to the booth and told the girl, "One of my relatives has a crush on you, but I can't tell you who it is because if he knew I had told you this much he would ring my neck."

The girl racked her brain trying to figure it out; she couldn't, so her mother told her she thought it was me. After the convention, the girl somehow got my phone number and called me about something arbitrary just to test out her mother's theory. When I answered the phone and heard her voice, I knew that it was now or never. After asking me the trivial question she called for, I got up the courage and asked her for a date. Two months later, I asked her to be my girlfriend.

Over the next year of dating Stephanie, I saw something very special in her. My standards were very high, and this was evident in the fact that she was only the third girlfriend that I had had in my life. She began to pass "quality assurance" on every standard that I had. I saw the same spiritual foundation in her as was in me. Her father was a godly pastor, and both of her brothers were ordained ministers. Her mother's spirit was magnetic both at home and work. Through situation after situation, I saw that the heart of Stephanie was like that of my mother. Little did I know that asking God for someone with a heart like my mother's would he give me both the heart and physical appearance of my mother. Stephanie looks more like my mother's daughter than I look like my mother's son.

After I had done much prayer and fasting, God gave me the spiritual confirmation that this was the woman whom I was supposed to marry. I bought her an engagement ring and decided to wait until my birthday to give it to her, but I couldn't wait that long (a month away). So I took her to a lake for a picnic on her birthday. I asked her to close her eyes, and I laid out a comforter on the grass and placed over a dozen roses—red, yellow, and pink—around the comforter and laid out a scrumptious picnic spread. As the sun set after the feast, I asked her if she was ready for dessert and handed her a handcrafted imitation ice cream sundae. Upon examination and after removing the fake ice cream, she found inside a jewelry box with the inscription "Desserts of the Heart." As she opened the box and removed the ring, I finally did what God placed on the sign above her head at that booth a year earlier: On one knee, I asked her.

Rules in James' House

TRAIN THEM UP	RULES I MUST OBEY
1. Pray every night and give thanks every morning. 2. Go potty, bathe, brush teeth, dress. 3. Say grace before eating. 4. Eat at table. 5. Put plates in sink. 6. Off to school. 7. Relax, play, stop when told. 8. No hitting or fighting. 9. Help your brothers and sisters. 10. Be kind and loving. 11. Pick up toys.	1. Say please when asking. 2. Say thank you when receiving. 3. Reward for obedience (deal). 4. Punish for disobedience (no deal). 5. Do homework. 6. Learn your scripture. 7. TV only when told. 8. Kiss Mommy and Daddy and Nanny; off to bed. 9. Take nap when not a school day. 10. Do good and good will come to you. 11. Be honest. Work hard. Keep good company.

Jeoshua Bronner, oldest son of James and Stephanie Bronner

The Household Mission Statement

There is a universal principle that sets up order in the household. All businesses have mission statements. Why not households? What follows is a mission statement that is used in our household. It may be used as an example for your household. Customize and use it for your family, and place it in an area of visibility for all family members to see and follow.

BRONNER FAMILY SITTING AT THE TABLE

Generic Model Mission Statement for Household

I. Objective: To learn the will of God for our lives and, to the best of our ability, to do it.

II. Priority System: In this family, we place God 1st, Family 2nd, and Business 3rd. Balance must be maintained between spirituality, family, finance, health, and helping others.

III. Organizational System:

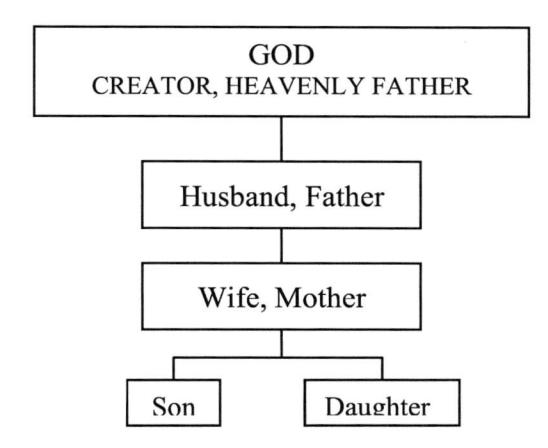

```
          GOD
CREATOR, HEAVENLY FATHER
           |
    Husband, Father
           |
     Wife, Mother
         /    \
       Son   Daughter
```

IV. Belief System: In this family, we believe there is only one true God. He is the God of Abraham, Isaac, and Jacob and the father of Jesus. We believe God sent his only begotten son, Jesus Christ, to come to earth to die for us. We believe Jesus is Lord. We believe he was crucified and God raised him from the dead so that our sins might be forgiven and we may experience everlasting life with Him. We believe the Bible is God's infallible Word and it is our guidebook and most trusted resource for life. We believe that God still performs miracles today. We believe in the trinity as one: God the Father; Jesus the Christ, His Son; and the Holy Spirit, His presence in the earth. We believe God desires a personal relationship with each of us and daily communion with him through prayer and worship and that reading his Word is required.

V. Destiny System: In this family, we believe that each of us has a destiny that we were born to perform. We believe the anointing of God's Holy Spirit will enhance our natural abilities and aid us in performing our destiny for the furthering of the kingdom of God. We believe that God is the head of this family and guides it, protects it, and gives favor to it. We believe that through prayer, faith, diligence, and obedience all things are possible. We believe we are sons and daughters of God; therefore, we are spiritual beings having a fleshly experience instead of fleshly beings having a spiritual experience. We believe that no amount of public success can compensate for failure at home. We believe there is no true success without God. We believe that God has blessed us to be a blessing to others. He has taught us to teach and multiplied our seed so that we may help cultivate the lost seeds of others. We believe that the will of God is above the desires and plans of men. We believe that we should use whatever ministry gifts placed within us to build and uplift the kingdom of God on earth as it is in Heaven. We believe we are only given one body so we should do all we can to preserve it through proper diet, exercise, and lifestyle. We believe in saving and not letting our spending exceed our income and investing those savings to get a return. We believe in having integrity in every area of our lives by demonstrating a spirit of honesty, faithfulness, diligence, and excellence.

_____   _____
Husband, Household President   Wife, Household Vice-Pres.

My very soul rejoices as our youngest son, James, coming out of our home, following the leadership of his father, knew exactly how to set his household in order. This household mission statement was designed by James as he knew every household needed a guide and needed to establish a belief system that will guide the family through the journey of life.

This was what he saw in our home and in the business. Mr. Bronner did not have to verbally teach the sons on bearing children. He taught them by example. James was the only son who not only matched his father with children but surpassed him.

Train up a child in the way he should go; and when he is old, he will not depart from it. (Prov. 22:6)

Thanks, James!

Chapter 8: The Business

Jesus said, **"Occupy (Do business) until I come."**

"In Him, we live, move, and have our being." (Acts 17:28)

God showed tremendous favor as we built a business and continued our first ministry: raising a family. His bloodline had established not only a commendable work ethic, but a pattern of thrift and sound financial management. His grandmother, Jane, had been freed from slavery with a bag of twenty-dollar gold pieces that she had managed to save. Later, she bought eighty acres of land. In her will, she left a parcel for each grandchild. Abraham's covenant was well in operation in the family long before Nathaniel and I began our journey. We only took up the mantle and saw to it that it was successfully delivered to the next generation.

Nathaniel and Arthur, Sr. worked long, hard hours servicing beauty salons across the country. They drove over country roads in all kinds of weather. As a result of their diligence, the business grew to a point that it was necessary to hire other people to help to carry the load. His mother reared Catherine, who finished Clark College and became his secretary. She worked for him all of her adult life.

They also hired many other individuals over the course of the years. Often times, they had no jobs available but created jobs just to help a struggling mother with children. On one occasion, Nathaniel met such an employee standing in the rain at a bus stop with a little girl. He stopped, gave her a ride, and brought her into the Bronner Brothers fold as a worker. She remained for over 30 years, her name, Lillie Roberts. He often said that people did not need employment, rather they needed development. Eventually, the company grew to over two hundred employees and approximately thirty individuals within the workforce were blood-related family members.

Meetings were convened on Tuesday mornings with all employees in attendance. It was here that he worked on implementation of successful business principles that made the company a force to be reckoned with in the beauty industry. This is an outline of typical in-store marketing/branding technique training. He offered these tips:

TOUCH your customer: the handshake.

HAND TEST: Allow the customer to feel the product.

HAND DELIVER: Increase your territory into new markets by going yourself!

WORKING HANDS: Hang signs for advertising (put BB magnetic signs on your vehicles).

HAND-IN: Balance your reports, budgets; maintain documentation.

OPEN HANDS: Honesty and loyalty keep a reputable business.

LAUNCHNG HANDS: Push! "A pro will have been kicked out of more establishments by 12 noon than an amateur will go in all day."

There is an old adage that says people are just like wheelbarrows: They will not go any further than you push them. To this end, he penned a favorite pep song. Anyone who ever worked at Bronner Brothers will always remember these lines:

Pep Song
We will set goals and deadlines,
We will set goals and deadlines.
We will set goals and deadlines
And get those goals on time.
You have to eye to buy it
You have to tell to sell it
You have to use sales hookers on those lookers
And those listeners.

He was a genius in leading the staff at the company in motivational exercises. These same principles were an overflow of the daily practices in our home. Our children and I were the first partakers. He also recognized the power of exposure. He brought in such noted personalities as Judge Ziglar, the brother of Zig Ziglar; Les Brown; Tony Brown; and Dick Gregory.

He was a mentor to many men of color in setting up beauty shop supply businesses. He gave scholarships to aspiring young people interested in the field of cosmetology.

I immediately found my place alongside my husband as his executive secretary. We worked long hours building the business. As I became better acquainted with procedures and the total operation, I moved to the position of bookkeeper. Because we were rearing a family, at first, I worked primarily from our home.

During the same time that our little family experienced rapid growth, our business ventures exploded with tremendous success. As can be expected with most businesses, we sometimes experienced times of challenge and mental anguish. There were times when cash flow was a serious issue. The company was growing. We had many demands upon us, including many families who depended upon us for income. We needed to purchase raw materials and equipment to keep our product lines running. We called upon our sister, Juanita Bronner Garmon, for expert assistance in management of our retail centers as well as artistic skills as a world-renowned hair weave technician and instructor. She also meticulously coordinated all BB International Beauty Show competitions, attracting stylists from around the world.

Our first Bronner Brothers Hair Show was held in 1947 at the historic Butler Street YMCA. At the completion of the writing of this book (Spring 2007), my sons and our family are about to celebrate sixty years of continuous service in the beauty industry. We have watched a lot of companies come and go over that period of time. We can only credit God for allowing us to remain in the marketplace. It was He alone who guided Nathaniel and Arthur through the early years. Later, He charted the course for all of the rest of the family as we moved together in business enterprise.

Remember to keep **God first**! He wants to teach us His ways. All we have to do is seek and ask Him and then just **do it**!

In 1991, the tremendous success of the company attracted the attention of *The World and I* magazine, a then very prestigious and massive publication based in Washington, D.C. The company and our family became the focal point of a feature article that circulated around the world. William Gordon, the award-winning writer, was born in a sharecropper's cabin in Mississippi. Relating well to the plight of two Black men, Nathaniel and Arthur, who entered the arena of business during an uncertain era, he managed to capture the best and worst aspects of their endeavors.

International Beauty Show

For sixty years, all of the BB International Beauty Shows have included prayer and thanksgiving. We were delighted to welcome approximately three hundred attendees at the first Bronner Brothers Beauty Show in 1947. They came to gain the latest information about the industry, to meet people related to the business, and to make purchases from our product line. Attendance has increased every year, causing us to change venues several times.

An Historical Overview

The birth of Bronner Bros. International Beauty Show began when Mr. Nathaniel H. Bronner, Sr. and his sister Emma Bronner conducted educational clinics in the Southeast region, teaching cosmetologists. The show progressed as follows:

1947-YMCA (downtown Atlanta): 300 cosmetologists were in attendance.

1955-Auburn Avenue Casino: Fabulous speakers joined the show. Jackie Robinson, the first African American to break the color barrier in baseball was a guest speaker. Dr. Martin L. King, Jr. was in attendance. The beauticians contributed over $1500 to help rebuild a burned Black church in Albany, Georgia.

1958-Atlanta City Auditorium: Dr. Benjamin Elijah Mays, president of Morehouse College, was the guest speaker.

1967-The Hyatt Regency Hotel: Bronner Bros. signed a ten-year contract with this new towering structure in downtown Atlanta.

1980's-Bronner Bros. expanded its show to include the Marriott Marquis and, later, to the Atlanta Merchandise Mart.

1990-The show was moved to the Atlanta Inforum.

1991-The show moved to The Georgia World Congress Center, and a ten-year contract was signed for this mammoth space.

1996-The show moved to Orlando, Florida, because of the Olympics in Atlanta and then went back to the World Congress Center.

1997-The Georgia World Congress Center: Exhibit space equates to over 350,000 square feet, attracts over 65,000 beauticians, 300 exhibitors, a fabulous fashion show, comedy hour, hair artistry contests, concert, educational seminars, Hair Battle Royale, church service, after parties, Gospel fest, and much more.

2007-Celebrating sixty years in business and still at the World Congress Center.

A Typical Experience at a BB International Fashion Show

FEEL THE EXCITEMENT!

Welcome to an exotic BB Fashion Show! There are glittering lights, smoke effects, dazzling fashions, and oops—there are legs!

Reminding us of the very first garden, we see Eve, simply clad. Before it's over, we'll fast forward all the way to Dolce & Gabbana and the height of present day fashion. Let's not overlook Eve's male companion in the progression. Yes, from Adam all the way to Versace!

> There are children born to skip and sway to a sassy beat – cute, unique, talented and on the move!
>
> They are prompted by velvet-voiced commentators who accentuate the evening with descriptive plays on fashion and words. Class announces itself as a neatly cropped white pedigree poodle parades down the runway. It swings along on a leash, controlled by a model just as chic! Both obviously have places to go. They're moving with real attitude.
>
> What's this? A hound dog on the loose with an equally naughty companion on its leash? This is a knock-out right on the runway! WOW!
>
> "Interruption please!" The commentator commands your attention. "It's time for the showcase. Are you ready for the most revealing and futuristic hair styles from around the globe?"
>
> The mood changes. Expectation fills the air. The music changes swiftly reflecting international variety. They are here—the most gifted platform artists in the world display an array of startling creations. The audience is on the edge of their seats as tresses are transformed into bird cages, mimic the Eiffel Tower, swirl like windmills, and blossom like tropical gardens. Once upon a time, it was just hair but not tonight!
>
> By now, there is standing room only as thousands cheer in total approval of unequalled fashion, creativity and talent at its absolute best—all on the BB stage!

Despise Not the Days of Small Beginnings

The founder Nathaniel Bronner, Sr. really started the business at age six in the country developing his skills in selling. (He also started his sons selling at age six).

Nathaniel, Sr. sold the Grit Newspaper, Cloverine Salve and brooder chickens. The selling gift was made evident early and transformed into bigger items as he grew and increased in wisdom and knowledge. I did not say money because it was a tool like anything else. If he could use wisdom and knowledge those credentials would opened the door to selling the right product at the right time and in the right places. As he moved to

Atlanta he sold fruit, Apex hair oils, ladies hosiery and the Atlanta Daily World Newspaper. He became the bus boy in a restaurant for provision until his business venture was well rooted. These were his early dabbling in the business of selling.

"What Are You Doing to Prepare the Next Generation to Take Over Bronner Bros.?"

The Nathaniel Bronner family sitting at the feet of a giant.

Dr. Benjamin E. Mays, the late President Emeritus of Morehouse College, seated in the center

The Institution of B₂B Continuity: A Piercing Question

The late Dr. Benjamin E. Mays, then President of Morehouse College, walked into the Bronner Super Beauty and Drug Center one day to see Mr. Bronner. Dr. Mays asked Mr. Bronner then (a graduate of Morehouse College) what he was doing to prepare the next generation of Bronners to take over. This was a piercing question. Dr. Mays went on to explain that he had seen two prominent Black business magnates who failed to prepare the next generation and their businesses died with them.

Mr. Bronner answered, "Be assured, I am preparing my sons. I am training them up in business everyday; I started them at six years old. This is how it's done…"

Work Ethics

1. At 5:30 a.m., they are up and on their *Atlanta Daily World* newspaper route before going to school. They learn how to sell subscriptions and make collections.
2. On weekends, they work in the drug store as cashiers, money order clerks, and stock clerks.
3. In summer months when school is out, they go on the beauty salon routes with our salesmen. We cover six surrounding southern states (North Carolina, South Carolina, Georgia, Florida, Alabama, and Tennessee) where they sell and deliver products to customers. They also work in the warehouse.
4. They sell our souvenir books at our International Beauty Shows.
5. They are taught to save their money: "A penny saved is a penny earned." They have savings accounts at the Wheat Street Baptist Church Credit Union. We do not give them allowances. They earn their own money; they work.
6. They are taught through experience self-employment.
7. Learning the customer is always right, we teach them honor and respect and how to be kind and considerate of others.
8. The first thing I look at on their report cards is CONDUCT. If the conduct is good, then their subject grades will be in order.
9. I take them to Bible study at Wheat Street under Dr. William Holmes Borders every Wednesday night and church on Sundays. This fortifies and stabilizes who they are. I am training them up in the business and the home while they are yet young.

Accountability Asks:
What Have You Done With The Talents I Have Given You?

Part I

In 1980, **a prayer room** was established at the BB Headquarters, 901 ML King Dr., and was moved to the new location, 600 BB Way, in 1982. The following outlines the journey that the first generation traveled as they established retail stores in the cosmetic field:

THE FIRST GENERATION OF BRONNER BROS.

NATHANIEL H. BRONNER, PRESIDENT

- 1947 Opened Business at 28 Butler Street.
- 1947 Established the International Beauty Show.
- 1956 Expanded to Beauty Center at 223 Auburn Ave.
- 1956 Expanded to Sister's Salon at 219 Auburn Ave.
- 1967 Expanded to Beauty Salon at 11 Ashby Street.
- 1969 Expanded to Drug Store at 911 Hunter Street.
- 1970 Expanded to Cosmetic & Wig Store at 103 Broad Street (downtown).
- 1971 Expanded to Cosmetic & Wig Store at 10 Broad Street (downtown).
- 1972 Expanded to Cosmetic & Wig Store at 33 Broad Street (downtown).
- 1972 Expanded to Cosmetic & Wig Store at West End Mall.
- 1978 Expanded to Beauty Center Retail at 899 MLK, Jr. Drive.
- 1978 Opened Manufacturing Plant at 110 Selig Drive.
- 1982 Opened Manufacturing Plant at 600 Bronner Bros. Way.
- 1987 Expanded to Beauty Center at 903 Hunter Street.
- 1987 Opened Manufacturing Plant on White Street.
- 1990 Expanded to Cottonwood Hot Springs Spa & Motel, Cottonwood, Alabama

Part II

God spoke to Joshua and said, **"Moses my servant is dead; now therefore arise, go over...as I was with Moses, so I will be with thee."** (Joshua 1:2-5)

God said to Bernard that Nathaniel, Sr., "My servant is dead; now therefore arise, look up, move onward, and possess the land."

To the next generation, God has said, "As I was with Nathaniel, Sr., so I will be with thee. Be strong and obey my commands."

THE SECOND GENERATION OF BRONNER BROS.
BERNARD BRONNER, PRESIDENT
(SINCE 1990)

- Paid off Cottonwood Hot Springs (Mr. Bronner's final request... debt free!) — 600 Hot Springs Road Cottonwood, Alabama

- Purchased upscale building. — Headquarters of Bronner Bros. and Upscale Magazine. 2141 Powers Ferry Road, Marietta (On I-285)

- Purchased Century Systems building. — Manufacturing Plant #3 120 Selig Drive, Atlanta

- Installed the 12-foot tall Hand Monument (Memorial Garden, honoring Nathaniel, Sr.). — 911 MLK, Jr. Drive, Atlanta

- Purchased Manufacturing Plant #4. — 4200 Wendell Drive, Atlanta

- Restored ancestors' properties (Homesteads and Cemeteries) — Kelly, GA and Forsyth, GA

- Consolidated three manufacturing plants into one. — 4200 Wendell Drive, Atlanta

- Expanded the International Beauty Show into Baltimore, MD, and the Seminars by the Sea to the Bahamas and surrounding islands. And continuing...

The Changing of the Guard

(Nathaniel Bronner and Bernard Bronner)

How His Father's Life's Lessons Guided Him

What we impart into our children is impacting. Be careful to sow good seeds and actions into the minds and hearts of your children.

It was 7:30 a.m. this morning when I heard a knock on my back door. "Who is it?" I asked.

"It's your son and it's cold outside." Hurriedly I ran to disengage the alarm system for him to enter.

Just flying in from California, Bernard made it to his mother's home to check on her after checking on his family. We live within walking distance, but this morning he was in his Jeep. He sat down and began to talk, reminiscing and trailing the route we had come and gleaned the successful events that made our beauty shows in the early years successful. He began, "Mother, I feel so good and excited over the changes instituted for the show this year. Do you realize we had discarded the very things that had made us successful? My father had instituted a souvenir yearbook for the hair show that remained in the beauty salons all year round. I remember the days we were eager to sell the books and make our own money. I was always the top seller. I worked while the other children were playing. Whenever they stopped to go swimming that was when I made my biggest sale. I let them play while I worked. That did something to me as a child and I recognized what it takes to get ahead.

"We are bringing back this year the souvenir books and we had a time trying to get the right catchy name for it. After giving approval to a name that I knew was not right, I was troubled in my spirit. I went to the barber shop for a hair cut. On my way home, it hit me like a lightening bolt...Fantasy! It was one word and that was my search. It was as if my father gave me that name. It was a call from the deep. I don't understand, but I know I am so programmed by my father's teachings and ways that I just knew that was the name he would have chosen at this time in history. So stay connected to the things you have learned, the things you have heard; and if there is virtue, praise, and trustworthiness in it, do it. I picked up my cell phone, called the office, and told them to stop the press. The new name shall be *Fantasy*. It will be a practical classroom for youth development in economic empowerment.

"You know, Mother, what I am going to do this year? I am going to take 'Little B' and train him how to sell souvenir books just as my father did all his sons, nephews, cousins, and employees' kids. 'Little B' is now five years old; and if I don't get him now and teach him how to sell, I will miss the golden opportunity for a lasting impression to do it by habit. It must grow up in him young and become habit forming early. Our lives are so impressionable at that age. I remember my father telling about the Catholic Church slogan, "Give me your child for the first six years and I will give him back to you for life." I know I have to teach him now all my selling skills and the very things that got me where I am today. I publish *Upscale* magazine because I saw from a child you and Daddy putting together the souvenir books around our dinning room table at night. You never know what impacts a child. My first magazine I published was *Smart Shoppers*. I started at home just as I had seen in my daddy. I transformed my basement into a magazine publishing company. It was there that my wife, Sheila, had a chance to use her Spelman

College degree with her computer skills to create work at home while nurturing the kids. I did not seek financing."

He jokingly laughed about how he had tried to get his mama to invest in his magazine and she turned him down. He later told me how he went home, sat on the bed with tears flowing down his face, telling God he could not get any help. He had no one but himself and God to get his magazine started. He did not realize then he had the right combination. Now he laughingly said he was so glad that no one invested in his magazine because he would have to pay big dividends today.

Bernard went on, "After the first year, I knew I did not have the right magazine nor the right name. It was then I came to my father and told him everything that I had tried was not working. I needed a new name. You remember the morning I walked over there? You were there working in the kitchen and Daddy was lying on the couch in the den. He was just listening to me talk. I told him about what was in the marketplace. I kept saying everything was 'upscale,' and I said it so much that Daddy jumped up and said, 'That's it!' I said, 'What?' He said, '*Upscale* magazine!' The rest is history. Today it is in its nineteenth year of publication. *Upscale* is housed in its own three-story office complex building on the I-285 perimeter in Marietta, Georgia."

Lesson: Dream and never give up; learn to turn a tiny seed into a mighty oak. Keep at it. Save your money. Bernard funded his own business from money made while servicing a beauty salon route as a young man in high school. He surprised me at age twenty-five when he married; he had saved $40,000.00 as a down payment on his home. Bernard had vision. At six years old, while servicing his paper route, he saw this house in our community and stood in front of it and said, "One day, I will own you." This is his house today.

Brother to Brother
(Article published in *Upscale* magazine)

When you do all you can and all you are supposed to do, people generally will appreciate you. I am happy to share a letter I recently received from one of my five brothers.

Dear Bernard,

I just want to commend you on how well you have been handling things since Daddy's death. I think you have been more than fair in the decisions you have made thus far. I like the positive changes you have made and continue to make in the business. I know Daddy is proud of you! Although I am not Daddy, I share his pride of you. When Daddy was in the hospital, you could tell how proud and confident he was of you by the way he responded. I can clearly understand Daddy's feelings over you. I believe he was able to see beyond where you were, at the time, to where you would be. The day before Daddy collapsed on his walk, he called me and assured me of my ability to handle the church. I thank God for that call and Daddy's pride and confidence in me.

I thank God for your maturity, balance, wisdom, and common sense. You have everything it takes to make a success of everything you touch! The Bible teaches, "Any enterprise is built by wise planning, becomes strong through common sense, and profits wonderfully by keeping abreast of the facts" (Prov. 24:3-4 TLB). While others are buying and building homes, you are building business. That's wisdom! I learned that from the Bible, too. "Develop your business first before building your house" (Proverb 24:27).

I trust what you are doing with Bronner Bros. and UPSCALE. It is my sincere prayer that the Lord will keep His hand upon your life and guide you every step of the way.

Well, I'm not going to preach in this letter. I just wanted to let you know that you have taken a formidable task and are handling it with great skill. I want to thank you for keeping a balanced head in business and for your diplomacy in handling people. You are doing a great job, and I believe that the best is yet to come!

May the Lord continue to be with you in all your endeavors and give you favor. I pray God's richest blessings upon you and your family!

In His Service,

Dale Bronner

This letter inspires me to do even more, and it lets me know people are watching and care. I believe that, in the words of my late father, I have done nothing special. I am just doing what I am supposed to.

Bernard Bronner

As It Was With Bernard, So It Was With Nathaniel, Jr.
(Nathaniel Starts His Own Business)

Coming home a college graduate with a degree in chemistry from Eckerd College, Nathaniel, Jr. proceeded to set up Bronner Bros. manufacturing plant. His father had just taken over a manufacturing plant that was in financial difficulty, God's perfect timing. Nathaniel was successful in setting up the operation, and his first product developed was the BB Cosmopolitan Curl, a highly successful product at the right time in the curl business.

The adventurous Nathaniel, Jr., with his massive mind had to keep on climbing, started his own business and was in need of a name. He asked me to pray about a name for his company. I did.

I saw it in a dream and told him the following day. "Your business shall be called Century Mortgage."

From the name Century, he incorporated the name Century Systems and Century Mortgage. Century Systems is for his current business, and Century Mortgage is for the future. His wife now holds a mortgage broker's license and a real estate broker's license.

Century Systems started as a business selling many different items from a garage door opener button to a book called *How to Eaves Drop on Your Neighbor*. I looked at the gadgets but never understood them nor bothered to even read his book. This was his early beginning. In fact, he set up the operation of his business at our home while James was still in high school. James was his chief bookkeeper and shipping clerk. They worked long hours each day, including Nathaniel's work as chemist and operations manager at the Bronner Bros. manufacturing plant.

Nathaniel said he would take his business to $50,000 a month and I said no way. Within a few years, he was selling $50,000 a week. I had to admit I limited him, but he did not receive that limitation. He changed what he was selling. I had to apologize after receiving that fantastic report. That is why it is important to build faith within the children early. He didn't give up; he changed what he was selling. He reached his goal by keeping on until he was selling the right product. Our children were so entrenched in selling it was hard for them not to sell. They were trained to sell early in their lives, and it became a pattern for whatever venture they pursued.

Nathaniel emphatically told me long ago that Century Systems was going to surpass Bronner Bros. I admit I gave him a little static on that, knowing he was really dreaming. Having high hopes, ambition, a scientific mind, research skills, salesmanship, being a chemist, and having a connection with his brother James had to work. I knew the call upon Nathaniel's life. He was different. He was gifted as a motivational speaker. His ministerial platform was in our early Tuesday morning staff meetings. He would stir your imagination, bring enlightenment, and leave you motivated. I often told him God had called him into the ministry. He would not listen to me. He said, "I am not going to preach."

I said, "Okay buddy, we will see." That is now history. Today he is Pastor Nathaniel.

James had now finished high school and had enrolled in Georgia Tech. While a student, he became involved in a company selling a product his father had once distributed. James dreamed his father came to him and told him to keep up the work he had begun with that company. James followed his dream and became the youngest five-star manager within one year in the company. His sales escalated so fast the company gave him trouble with his orders and sales. He knew after two years it was time to make a change and use those selling skills for himself in his own company. He carried all his skills to his big brother and partner in Century Systems. They developed their first nutritional product called Eden's Fruit. It sold in several health food stores. The product gained attention in the market place, and soon Nathaniel was sued for the use of the name Eden's Fruit. He lost over $40,000 fighting that case. God had warned him in the beginning that he would spend that amount in the case.

Nathaniel had to experience that episode. Nothing is lost if you keep the right attitude about what happens to you. There is another adage, "If you pay for an experience, keep the receipt." God allowed him to make his mistake while he was yet growing to prepare him to take the storms ahead. One of his biggest vendors put him through hard knocks, but he understood it was still a part of his journey if he wanted to be successful and make mega bucks.

Remembering his prophetic announcement of a product on his drawing board that would escalate above the sales of Bronner Bros. kept his ambition high while working to release that product. Today, Century Systems is located in its own manufacturing plant on Selig Drive in the Fulton Industrial Blvd. area of Atlanta.

Lesson: Nathaniel worked hard and paid tithes while still in high school. He learned to tithe to his own brother Dale and no one knew it. He gave proceeds to his other brothers who were not as prosperous as he and Bernard every month. I nearly shed tears when I discovered the large monthly sum he gave his brothers from his company. I told him as a man once told me, "Your breadbasket will never go empty. Give and it shall be given unto you, good measure, pressed down, shaken together and running over." A divine principle: Charity starts at home, then spreads abroad.

Nathaniel wanted to make his own money while in college. I remember the day he called his dad to ask if he could go and apply for a job at Kmart. His dad's response was, "Create your own job. You have all of the beauty and barber shops in Florida. I'll have the products shipped to you. You go and sell!" That was the answer that he needed. Nathaniel made up to $500 a week after creating a route in the Tampa area. This became his fascinating dream and inspired him to want to expand more and more.

How to Start Your Own Business

Since the first printing of this book, one of the questions people would often ask of me after I did a public speech is, "How do I start my own business?" This is a complex process that takes research, discipline, determination, drive, a good idea and much hard work. The best book I can recommend on the subject that will give you all of the tools you can get from a book is Entrepreneur Magazine's "Start Your Own Business: The Only Start-Up Book You'll Ever Need." At the time of this writing, that book is in its fourth edition. The book starts with a test to determine how well you fit the mold for entrepreneurship. The very first thing you need to learn is not the technique but whether you are cut out to have your own business.

In addition, you can write the Bronner Business Institute - Kingdom Connections Networking - The Word of Faith Life Training Center - 108C 212 Riverside Parkway, Austell, Ga. 30168. For more info visit www.nhbbi.org.

Chapter 9: Health and Physical Activities

In Mr. Bronner's travel to Florida at Panama City Beach, he noted a signpost at a church that read "Dr. Hoffman of California Guest Speaker Tonight for Health Seminar."

Needless to say, Mr. Bronner arrived ahead of time; and I am sure he was the only man of color there. Dr. Hoffman had spent three months in Hunzaland studying the people, the land, and longevity enjoyed by that population. He discovered that people died of old age and not of disease. There was no crime, no policemen, and no need of hospitals; this was their way of life. They grew their own food and lived a peaceful lifestyle. Of course, they did not have lavish homes and automobiles like Americans. They lived up in the hill country with rolling terraced gardens. Among a list of fresh fruits and vegetables, they claimed apricots as the key food of longevity.

Mr. Bronner's humble style led him to Dr. Hoffman's wife to secure the information needed to engage him in Atlanta for people of color. One of Dr. Hoffman's criteria was it must be held at a church. Mr. Bronner called Rev. Larry Williams of the Zion Hill Baptist Church, within walking distance from our home, who gladly opened his doors for the seminar. Mr. Bronner made it a community project.

The very first night, Dr. Hoffman said, "The key to good health is if you keep your blood stream clean, alkaline, and free-flowing with plenty of oxygen, you will never get sick; and if you are sick, you will get well. Now, let's throw away our coffee pots, salt and pepper shakers, all condiments, greases, white flour, white sugar, red meats, our cigarettes, and let's begin to live." Well, that was perceived as too difficult for many and they turned a deaf ear; but there were those who were sick and wanted to get well. It was the few who kept coming night after night.

Long, sleek, and slender in body, Mr. Bronner was always seeking a way for healthful living, not only for his family but for other people as well. He taught whatever he knew to his staff every Tuesday morning with great joy.

Our family planned two trips per year, one to the Natural Hygiene Society Conventions, where we were the only family of color in those days, and the other to beaches, mainly Panama City Beach, Florida. We traveled in a Volkswagen camper with all the equipment as we enjoyed our routine of stopping along the highway. Later, we were able to buy several condos on beautiful Panama City Beach. In our research on the name Bronner, meaning "one who dwells by the spring," we could understand why Mr. Bronner had a longing for the water: It was a part of his destiny.

Cottonwood Hot Springs

His longing for the water led him to Cottonwood Hot Springs in Cottonwood, Alabama. Cottonwood had come to be known as the site of a facility that performed chelating therapy. Individuals with cardiac problems sought this treatment as an alternative to bypass surgery. The facility included a complete clinic and lodging for the patients. There were certified medical doctors and nurses on staff. An added bonus to the treatment was the wonderful healing waters of nature's 112-degree hot salt mineral springs, flowing from approximately a mile underground. The water flowed into two outdoor pools and eight interior mineral baths. There were also a restaurant, conference center, worship center, and a lake for fishing, along with paddleboats, on the seven hundred acres of land.

In his usual quiet method, Mr. Bronner went to the wife of the doctor/owner and asked her to please inform him if her husband ever decided to sell the property. He wanted the first opportunity to purchase the entire facility. She assured him that if they decided to sell that he would be the absolute first person they would contact. In approximately one year, the property was for sale; and he was contacted just as they had promised. The initial asking price was enormous and Mr. Bronner declined. The property was sold to another buyer, who later ended in foreclosure. This was Mr. Bronner's perfect opportunity to buy. Dick Gregory became the connector and informant at this point.

God works in many wonderful ways! At the end of the scenario, Mr. Bronner became the owner of the facility. We knew that the facility would be used for building and rebuilding family relationships, healthful living, and rejuvenating retreats. We knew that its purpose was to provide a holistic program for those who would visit during our ownership. Many individuals visited the facility. Some drove for hundreds of miles. Some drove across state lines every week to bathe in the mineral waters and enjoy the peace, quiet, and healthy food. It was a favorite getaway for our children, many senior citizens groups, Christian organizations, our employees, and our extended family.

Cottonwood had long been a health-restoring resource for the people of Cottonwood and nearby Dothan, Alabama. It also brought economic vitality to this small town. Mr. Devon Brown of Jamaica served as the supervisor and manager of the facility. Juanita Bronner Garmon served as the official hostess of the facility. She graciously welcomed guests on behalf of our family on a regular basis. She especially enjoyed leading fitness segments and teaching senior citizens to swim. Juanita was ably assisted by our brother-in-law, Mr. Henderson Lewis, a retired salesman with Bronner Bros. He served at different times in the capacity of chef, along with Minnie McGriff and Harriet Johnson Pitt. He also served as chauffeur and Chief of Security. He did so with special release and encouragement from his loving wife, Annie Lee Lewis. In 2001, after ten years of operation, the facility burned to the ground.

We intend to rebuild. The healing mineral waters continue to flow from the earth as God intended. We are still in full ownership of this part of the earth and will restore it to greater beauty than before.

Sins of the Heart: Jealousy

Wellness is not only affected by our physical environment and foods we eat but by those things we take to heart. Lying in bed at my mother's home many years ago early in the morning, I listened to a sermon by a minister on the Seventh Day Adventist Hour. He pointed out that anytime the Holy Spirit has been tugging at you concerning something you are holding in your heart, you then need to adhere to and cleanse it from your heart.

The Holy Spirit gave me the word *jealousy* concerning a person. The minister pointed out that if you ignore it, you are rejecting the Holy Spirit. The Holy Spirit is there to convict us of our sins. If you turn Him away after several warnings, you indeed reject Him and there is no more help for you. You have turned your help away. When I heard those words, a thunderbolt-like feeling hit me and I said, "Yes Lord, I don't want to reject the Holy Ghost. I will call and face her with my feeling."

I tried to reach her by telephone but to no avail. I confessed my sin to God; and later arriving home; I called and told her to be in the Thursday night's Bible class. I called my prayer partner to inform her I was in town. She was silent for a few minutes then began sobbing. Afterward, she said, "The Lord says read Romans 5:19." Remember, I had not mentioned one thing to my prayer partner; neither did she know what was going on in my life, but the Holy Spirit did. Look at how God spoke to me. Romans 5:19 reads as follows:

For as by one man's disobedience many were made sinners, so by the obedience of one shall many be made righteous.

The entrance of God's word brought a holy boldness to me. I rose up before the class that night and made an open confession of jealousy to her and asked for forgiveness. Something strange followed; people all over the class got up and made open confessions of jealousies they held with each other. Some testimonies involved people who were not in the class. It ushered in a total cleansing, beginning with my confession. It brought light to the second part of the same scripture: **"By the obedience of one shall many be made righteous."**

Afterwards, many people came to me saying they did not know why I was jealous of her. It wasn't for them to figure out! I kept my focus on doing what I had to do, and the rest was left to the Holy Spirit. I knew God was using me to show the way of cleansing not only for myself but for others that they might heed these inward feelings and cleanse them.

And when ye stand praying, forgive, if ye have ought against any: that your Father also which is in heaven may forgive your trespasses." But if ye do not forgive, neither will your Father which is in heaven forgive your trespasses. (Mark 11:25-26)

That is a very meaningful scripture, and Jesus saw fit to speak the words as He taught.

Years later, a second jealousy spirit entered. At that instant, something hit the pit of my stomach. I said, "Oh, God, what was that?" He let me know it was the spirit of jealousy. I said to myself, "Not again." This time I knew what to do. I called the person and told her of the incident. Not only did I tell her; but in our staff meeting, I got up and shared the jealousy testimony. Again, many others made similar confessions. I have testified that, when I detect a spirit of jealousy or hatred within my spirit, I have gone back to the people and made an open confession. This is a part of my calling to be a light to so many others. Some people are full of inward or hidden sins that only God sees, and He will bring them to light. I know people who use the excuse, "I don't go back to the person; I go to God." Yes, I go to God; but in every case where I have made open confessions, so many other people have been helped.

Whenever I recognize my error, I move quickly to stop it before it grows into something bigger. I pray that, as I share my spiritual experiences, someone will be helped to go and do likewise. Sins of the heart must be cleared, and God only knows the heart.

The Lying Spirit

God watches our every action, even on things we might consider small. It is said we have to give an account of every idle word. I have told many big ones, so much so that I considered this one small; but it got God's attention and mine.

One summer day, my granddaughter was visiting. Admiring a pair of small earrings I was wearing, she asked for them. I removed them and gave them to her. Sitting on the sofa playing, she dropped the earrings and couldn't find them. She asked me if I had seen them and I said no. Actually, I had found them and placed them in my pocket. Later, her mom came and the very first thing my granddaughter said again was, "I lost my earrings and can't find them." I knew they were in my pocket but never said so. I had given them away but was trying to hold on to what I had given. That was wrong. In addition, I did not tell the truth. That was a deceitful heart and a lying tongue.

Later that night, I went to Word of Faith School of the Word. As I walked down the aisle, the scene of Isaiah 6:5 flashed when Isaiah appeared before God and said, **"Woe is me! for I am undone; because I am a man of unclean lips, and I dwell in the midst of a people of unclean lips: for mine eyes have seen the King, the Lord of hosts."**

Conviction hit and I said, "I lied to my granddaughter." I asked God's forgiveness; but the next day, I called her mom and told her the incident and apologized to my granddaughter and gave her those earrings. I explained to her what her grandmother had done. These things might seem small; but in God's sight, this was a heart condition.

Fibroid Tumor through Uterus

During the birth of my fourth son, Dale, came the growth of a grapefruit size tumor. Excessive bleeding resulted monthly. The Doctor informed me to have the baby and afterwards it would be necessary to remove the uterus. That was disturbing news to me because I wanted more children. Had I listened to the doctor, I wouldn't have had Charles, James or ten of my grandchildren. That decision affected twelve beings. I persevered month after month with excessive bleeding and cramps but refused to have my uterus removed. I could feel the tumor by just pressing the abdomen. I searched and searched for a natural way to rid me of the tumor. I found in a Medical self help book if the tumor did not bother you, don't you bother it. Other than the menstrual cycle I had no problems.

Nathaniel, Jr. asked me to go on a seven day water fast with him about four years later. I had only been four days with just water. I knew I also suffered with stomach ulcers and to go seven days without food would aggravate the stomach to unbearable. I prayed and prayed as I started this journey. I was mentally prepared and ready to go. I could tell I was being divinely led because I had no problems. At day six, suddenly, I suffered from the ulcer and had to break the fast.

Approximately two weeks later without thinking or noticing anything, one of our employees needed medical attention but was afraid to go to the Doctor. As an encourager, I booked an appointment for both of us. We had to fill out paper work on our health issues and I listed the fibroid tumor through the uterus.

After the examination the Doctor said, "I found no tumor". I said excuse me, would you repeat that? He repeated, I found no tumor and he left the room. Oh my God! Oh my God! I said with thanksgiving to God for using Nathaniel, Jr. to lead me into those six days not seven, water fast. I could see that the tumor was diet related and could be controlled by diet.

Nathaniel later wrote a book about Fasting and it is available free to read at QuickFasting.com.

Chapter 10: Education

Home Schooled First

A, B, Cs - Always Be Certified From God

The home is the first school of learning. It is here that children learn from example. "If your parents don't teach you, the world will" was my husband's frequent expression. I encourage parents to **teach**, **correct**, **build**, and **demonstrate**. It is during the formative years that the "hands on" experience becomes their first process. They learn from doing and from what they see or hear. The following was made clear by my granddaughter, Christina, when she gave me and her dad a copy of this quote.

> **To hear is to forget,**
> **To see is to remember, but**
> **To do is to understand.**

Author Unknown

	THE BUILDING BLOCKS
VISION	Without vision, the people perish—not because they lack knowledge but because they reject knowledge
GRATITUDE	When we do a mental and spiritual inventory of all we have, we realize that indeed we are very rich. Learn to say, "Thank you." It doesn't hurt. That same appreciation opens the door to **abundance**.
CHARACTER	Keep in mind a reputation is hard to achieve, but in an instant it can be quickly destroyed.

SIMPLICITY	The desire to clear out, think through, and carefully analyze the essentials of what is needful to live well—this will bring contentment. We are hard to satisfy. The more we see, the more we want. "Be content, whatsoever the state," says Paul the Apostle. (Appreciate what you have!)
ORDER	Internally first, then moving to the external, brings harmony. That breeds inner peace and opens the door to joy. Order is the first law of creation.

As our sons entered high school, I rewarded them for every A on their report card. I used this as an incentive for them to become honor roll students. It helped them to strive for the best. All of their abilities did not manifest in the same way, so I made adjustments to pull up the enthusiasm of the child who needed an additional boost. For example, I told one son that if he made all A's that I would give him $200. This was exciting and a real challenge. Reflecting on his past struggles, he responded, "Shoot!" We had a lot of fun and laughter with this. It stirred up his zeal and caused him to want to do better than he had before.

Both of us were college graduates. Mr. Bronner offered his sons no less than an earned degree. The standard was already set. To require any less of our sons would have represented failure of responsibility as a parent.

Understanding that earning a degree was not optional, all of our sons enrolled in colleges or universities, and they all graduated! We adopted the Bumblebee Attitude. You see, the bumblebee had no idea that it was virtually impossible to lift its comparatively large body with such small wings. One of our sons had problems, but he persevered. Even with these difficulties, he was programmed from our home to finish college. By the time he graduated, he jokingly said he felt as if he had a PhD. It wasn't a doctorate degree; however, he was a college graduate. That was all that we required!

Nathaniel Hawthorne, Jr.: Graduate of Eckerd College, St. Petersburg, Florida. He was the first African American to graduate with a degree in chemistry from this institution. He presently serves as vice president and heads the manufacturing division of Bronner Bros. Company. He is president and founder of Century Systems Inc. at TheWoman.com, a company that manufactures natural health products. Nathaniel is the pastor of The Ark of Salvation and founder of the AirJesus.com website, which includes MountainWings.com, which became the world's largest inspirational e-mail with over one million subscribers.

Bernard Holmes: Graduated from Georgia State University, Atlanta, with a degree in accounting and finance. He's president and CEO of Bronner Bros. Co. and is owner and publisher of *Upscale* magazine. Bernard is an associate of Rainforest Films.

Darrow Wendell: Graduated from Morehouse College, Atlanta, with a degree in business administration. He served as show director and director of the Professional Sales Division of Bronner Bros. Company. He made his transition on February 6, 2000, at age thirty-eight.

Dale Carnegie: Graduate of Morehouse College, Atlanta, with a degree in religion and business. He received honors as the highest ranking student in the School of Religion from Morehouse. Dale received a Doctorate of Ministry degree from The Christian Life School of Theology. Initially, he worked in Bronner Bros. as manager of the computer department. Dale is in full-time ministry as bishop and senior pastor of Word of Faith Family Worship Cathedral with over 15,000 members.

Ministries that have been birthed out of Word of Faith Cathedral are

1. Word of Faith Love Center, Rev. Reginald Garmon, pastor
2. Word of Faith Light and Joy, Rev. Frank Salters, pastor
3. The World Overcomers Ministries, Jackson, Mississippi, Rev. Leyonn Armstrong, Pastor
4. The Community of Faith Church, Gwinnett County, Georgia, Rev. Tony Moore, Pastor

Charles Elijah: Graduate of Morehouse College, Atlanta, with a degree in banking and finance. He is presently the finance officer of Bronner Bros. Charles is co-pastor of The Ark of Salvation, Atlanta, and minister of The Weekend Word television program, recorded live on

Friday evenings from 7:00 p.m. to 8:00 p.m. at The Ark and aired live on AirJesus.com.

James Stanley: Graduate of Georgia Tech University, Atlanta, with a degree in computer engineering. He is manager of the Information Technology Department for Bronner Bros. Company and vice president of Century Systems. He is pastor of the youth ministry at The Ark of Salvation and technical director for the AirJesus.com websites.

All of our sons pursued specialized training in college that supported our business. This helped to refine business processes and helped us to remain competitive in an international market. A wise father required such deposits back into the family company's enterprise.

In a recent conversation, Bernard, our second son, now president of the company, revealed some statistics he found alarming and an indicator of the importance of gaining an education. He told me that 80% of all young men sentenced to prison enter without a high school diploma. In years past, he has generously supported higher education and made donations to help educate young people in college. Now, in addition to supporting college efforts, he feels it is time to look at what he describes as "lower education."

Bernard plans to launch an all-out campaign to help young people considered at-risk to gain a high school diploma. This is the area in which he sees the greatest need as he surveys joblessness, crime, family matters, and many other challenges. He is the father of five children ranging from elementary school age through college. His immediate plans include helping 10,000 young people with special challenges to finish high school. He considers this his special call.

World Mission: Bearing Precious Seed

The Great Commission: "Go ye into all the world and preach the gospel" (Mark 16:15). (Also referenced in Matthew 28:19)

In 1982, as a youth, Dale and I traveled to the Holy Land where he baptized all seventeen in our group in the river of Jordan. In 2006, three of my sons, Dale, Nathaniel and Charles, traveled to Ukraine, the former USSR, to conduct leadership and business training seminars.

Dale has conducted leadership training seminars as bishop and the chairman of the board of the Christian Men's Network, founded by the late Dr. Edwin Louis Coles. These ministerial leadership training seminars have taken place in Austria, Canada, Columbia, El Salvador, England, Guatemala, Honduras, Bolivia, Panama, Peru, South Africa, Venezuela, and also Fiji, the farthest point from Jerusalem on the face of the earth.

The purpose of the ministerial leadership seminar is to train 1,000 trainers to reach 25,000 other pastors and leaders. From horseback, as old circuit riders of their ancestors, to jet planes today, they have traveled carrying the Gospel and bearing precious seed.

> **For as the rain cometh down, and the snow from heaven, and returneth not thither, but watereth the earth and maketh it bring forth and bud, that it may give seed to the sower, and bread to the eater: So shall my word be that goeth forth out of my mouth: it shall not return unto me void, but it shall accomplish that which I please, and it shall prosper in the thing whereto I sent it. (Isaiah 55:10 – 11)**

GO, GO, GO!

The harvest is plentiful, but the laborers are few. (Matthew 9:37)

Chapter 11: The Missing Link

This is why Mr. Bronner chose the hand to teach life's lessons. The hand turns time. The dictionary describes the hand as a source of aid, help, guidance, instruction, applause, promise to marry, possession, or care. It is the grandparents' hand that has the power to mold an entire generation. There is a nurturing hand that is placed in the hand of God that shapes and molds children and grandchildren. There is a special glue and a binding stitch that keeps the family from unraveling. It is a tie that forever binds.

After one generation reaches the age of fifty, its responsibility then becomes to reach back and show the oncoming generation the right path. It is that generation's responsibility to help with the roadblocks, the detour signs that will invariably come along, the dangerous curves on the highway of life, and the bridges that have been washed away. There will be times when the younger generation must travel at their own risk, but it is the hand of the older generation that should help direct them to the straight yet narrow path.

The Mighty Oak Tree

Grandparents are to be the mighty oak tree: watering, planting, cultivating, and preparing the grandchildren to weather the tests of life. Grandparents must help strengthen the roots for the grandchildren to grow into mighty oaks.

Grandchildren need to be made responsible children through the molding of habits and thoughts so they can grow academically and spiritually. We know that the grandparents' first responsibility was to train up their own children, teach, and guide them in the right paths so they might be strengthened to teach their children, allowing grandparents to fill in with outstretched arms for the perfecting of the finished product.

Grandma's Boot Camp

My answer to the demand for a strong figure to guide the next generation was a boot camp for my grandchildren. At my invitation, seven moved into my house for a time of special bonding or molding.

We went back to the old way of doing things. They were in bed by 9:30 p.m. and up before dawn at 5:30 a.m. There was prayer and praise at 6:00 a.m. and breakfast at 6:45 a.m. The six older kids had their lunches prepared by 7:15 a.m. and were off to work at 7:30 a.m. At 4:00 p.m., the working kids were back home; there was rest and relaxation at 4:20 p.m., dinner at 5:00 p.m., on their own at 6:00 p.m., and at 9:30 p.m. they were ready for bath and bedtime. It was fun—they were exhausted! I made sure that there was a go-cart, trampoline, scooters, swing sets, and a basketball goal. My yard resembled that of a small park with a brook running across the front. We even had an organized game of soccer with cousins Delores Harmon as coach and her son, Joshua Harmon, as referee.

On Sundays, they were taught to tithe out of their paychecks: giving God his due first. On weekends, some of the grandchildren went home and others stayed; and on Sunday night, they were all back in place. Finally, on the last weekend of the summer during family reunion, we all went on a seven-day cruise to St. Martin and St. Thomas. I was delighted that one grandchild decided to stay with me as she prepared for college.

One of the highlights of the summer was when their Uncle Dale came over and brought a graduation gift for one of the grandchildren graduating from high school and a personal journal book for another grandchild who had been attending his teen meetings. On that night, Dale touched the grandchild whom he presented the journal, not knowing through his touch, God had begun to do amazing work on this grandchild. This took place around 9:00 p.m.

Later that night, around midnight, I heard a whisper going on in the great room. I was amazed to see that the Holy Spirit was dealing with my grandchild. I quietly tiptoed in and took a seat to observe what was going on. Her hands were uplifted and she was dedicating her entire life to Christ. She began shaking with tears flowing and rapid-fire words coming from her mouth. This experience lasted until 2:30 a.m. the next morning. I couldn't move and silently sat thanking God for this transformation of my grandchild. I know now that God orchestrated my summer that year and sent the grandchildren to spend time with me. We were one big happy family, and I will never forget this most amazing summer. I thank God for Jane Bronner, who came to assist me.

My grandchildren are growing up with wonderful work ethics, and all have purposed to work with the family company every summer and change departments every summer until they have worked every phase of the business. They are planning now how they can better the company and how Cottonwood can be restored. I am so very proud of them; and as I listen to their future plans, I know that my job as a grandmother has served its purpose. By precept and example, they are learning to become leaders of tomorrow.

Lesson: Tough times never last; only tough people do. Teach your children to have their own ideas, only you shape them. Arm them with ammunition to fight through the tough times. If there is not an opened door, create one.

This was the agenda for Grandma's boot camp:

5:30 a.m.   Arise.

6:00 a.m.   Prayer and Praise

Exercising to praise music barefoot on the front lawn. I made sure no insecticide was sprayed on the lawn. (Remember Mr. Bronner's theory that healing properties were in the dew and absorbed through the bottom of the feet). Careful attention to early morning sounds—birds chirping, frogs croaking, and intermittent silence—and a visual appreciation of the sunrise, a quiet unfolding event.

6:45 a.m.   Breakfast

A special menu for the children working at the company (e.g., grits, veggie sausage links, bacon, eggs, wheat toast, orange juice, water, and soy milk).

7:15 a.m.   Lunches Ready

Turkey, cheese, lettuce, tomatoes on wheat bread, spread, chips, fruit punch, and fruit. Off to work at the company!

7:30 a.m.   Beginning

The work days begins.

4:00 p.m.   Home from Work

Rest and relaxation

5:00 p.m.   Dinner

(Example: Green beans, broccoli, baked chicken, rice, yams, and cornbread)

6:00-9:00 p.m. Fun Time

9:30 p.m.   Bath and Bedtime

(They were exhausted!)

A Letter from My Granddaughter

I've tried to do my part as a grandparent by providing both a nurturing hand and a hand of discipline. Here is a letter that I received from one of my grandchildren after being with me in boot camp.

Dear Grandmother:

This year has been a wonderful blessing and a great transformation for me. Thanks to you, I have learned how to appreciate the things that many people overlook or take for granted. I have learned to be thankful and grateful, and my eyes have been opened to see God's great love. Grandma's Boot Camp really made a difference in my life. Thanks a lot for the blessings, prayers, teachings and meals that you placed upon me. I look forward to the next session of Grandmother's Boot Camp. You are a true angel!!! Someday, I'm going to be just like you; having great impacts on others' lives.

Love,

Christina

2002

After reading this beautiful letter, I could only say, "Oh, how wonderful it is to be a grandmother!"

The Story of the Hand Tree

It was Grandparent's Day, November 25, 2003, at Whitefield Academy where four of my grandchildren attended. The fifth grade class of Joy Bronner (Darrow and Jane Bronner's child) did a presentation of the tree with the handprints. The principal, Dr. Bill Seronello, did a lecture on the oak tree.

As I was sitting in the auditorium looking and listening, a thought registered in my mind: You need to do the tree of hands for all the Bronner grandchildren of James and Emma Bronner. Yes, I'll do it! I got so excited and later began to call the different Bronner families to finger paint all the grandchildren's hands to wave on the family tree for that Christmas. Instead of a Christmas tree, I would do a Family Tree for Christmas. I knew the perfect person to draw the tree and connect the hands, Ms. Felida Neily, a talented Bronner Bros. employee.

Hands from Chicago, Washington, D.C., Florida, North Carolina, Maryland, and Georgia came in—all in different colors and shapes—making the tree excitingly attractive. The only surviving Bronner ancestor was Mr. A. E. Bronner. Eighty-nine years old at the time, he and his wife, Ann Bronner, were there at the Christmas dinner celebration in my home. What a celebration!

All the small children sat on the floor to look, listen, learn, and participate in the program. Descendents from each of the twelve branches on the tree gave the historical sketch of their parents, lit a candle, and held the stone with the ancestor's name written thereon. Following was a money book presentation to all the children who had not previously received a book. The money book contained twelve $1 bills with the letters A to L in the seal that represented the twelve Federal Reserve Districts, a silver Susan B. Anthony dollar, a $2 bill with commentary on the mints and the Federal Reserve Districts. It is a keepsake collection and will teach each child to save money. The children sang, danced, and recited Scriptures. It was a meaningful, fun day on Christmas 2003.

THE HAND TREE

My Grandmother

The Hand Tree was a fifth grade project at Whitefield Academy (11-25-2003) for Grandparents' Day where my granddaughter, Joy Bronner attends. She introduced me to her 5th grade class. This is what she said:

Hi! I am Joy Bronner and I have the privilege of introducing Mrs. Robbie Bronner. She is one of my grandmothers. My grandma is very special. God has brought her a long way. She has been through and knows what hard times are; however, she also knows what good times are. Good times are when you experience the blessings of God.

One of her testimonies is that one day she was running to turn the alarm off inside her house when she slipped, fell, and hit her head on the glass table in her kitchen. She didn't get cut, but one of the men who were picking up the glass was cut from it. God tested her faith. She always has faith in God. She is a godly woman.

My grandma's house is filled with angels. My grandma loves the Lord with all her heart. She is blessed by God every step of the way. She knows whom to call on for help. God is always with her.

My grandmother is so sweet. She gives food and money to the homeless, and she's nice to a lot of people. She makes lots of friends, and she loves the world.

My grandparent is so lovely. She cares for all of her grandchildren. She loves me very much and she's so nice to me. She also cooks very well! I love her!

I now introduce to you Mrs. Robbie Bronner.

***

And all thy children shall be taught of the Lord; and great shall be the peace of thy children. (Isaiah 55:13)

Grandchildren: Twenty-Nine and Growing

(12 Boys and 17 Girls)

Nathaniel, Jr.	4 boys: Nathaniel III, Josees, Christian, and George
Bernard	5 children (4 girls and 1 boy): Christina; Ashley; Nicole; Brianna; and Bernard, Jr.
Darrow	5 children (2 boys and 3 girls): Robie; Jarvis; Kimberly; Darrow, Jr.; and Joy
Dale	5 children (4 girls and 1 boy): Dalina, Neiel, Kirstie, Kristie, and Dale II.
Charles	3 children (2 girls and 1 boy): Amaris; Elisha; and Charles, Jr.
James	7 children (3 boys and 4 girls): Jeoshua, John, Joseph, Jamie, Jenesis, Jasmine, and Jade

A seed shall serve Him. It shall be accounted to the Lord for a generation. (Psalm 22:30)

PORTRAIT OF THE GRANDCHILDREN

They shall come and shall declare His righteousness unto a people that shall be born that he hath done this. (Psalm 22:31)

Grandchildren's Destiny Statements

I asked my grandchildren the question, "Do you know your purpose or destiny in life?" Their responses were as follows:

NAME	AGE	DESTINY STATEMENT
1. **Robie**	23	My life's purpose is to educate, inspire, and encourage children who have been emotionally and physically abused. I would like to work with the physically and mentally challenged with special emphasis on the hearing impaired. Lastly, I would like to open a facility that caters to all their needs.
2. **Dalina**	21	A music teacher and performing artist.
3. **Jarvis**	21	I have all faith in God that the purpose He has placed on my life is to be a leader to those who are wondering, a mentor to those in need, and a friend to those who are friendless. I attend Bethune-Cookman University and I am the senior class president and the vice president of the NAACP chapter on campus.
4. **Christina**	20	Destiny to me is similar to the fingerprints of God. Everyone has his or her own different, unique, and spiral pattern. Through these patterns, we are linked to our family values, spiritual praises and financial limitations. God has determined the essence of our destiny. This happened long before we were introduced to society. God creates our destiny and determines its form, size, shape, and character. As I move toward even greater maturity,

		I am still involved in the quest for a true understanding and enlightenment as to what my destiny is and its deepest meaning. For now, I see my destiny as I see a sponge. The most striking characteristic of a sponge is its capacity to take in and soak up plenty of things, substances, and especially water. But what makes it even more interesting is that at the right time, it can be squeezed to give it all back. As God showers me with a multitude of gifts and blessings of love, patience, grace and mercy, family and friends, lifelong lessons, money and much more, I soak it in, ready for any time upon which I will be squeezed to release it all back to His people. I strive to give back to the world a portion of what God has given to me.
5. Neiel	19	I believe that I am here to simply make a difference by leaving a legacy to others. Helping others in any way that I can is my desire. I want to help change lives all over the world by impacting others through my writing. I know that I am destined to write multiple best selling books—novels, self-help, and informational type books. I will also be a news broadcaster or something of the like.
6. Ashley	17	To be a successful CEO of a business foundation making millions of dollars to pour back into my community. Also, as a teenager to encourage and inform young Black teens of the importance of postponing sexual involvement.
7. Kimberly	17	I believe that my purpose is to work hard, have fun, and honor God in everything that I do.

8. Nicole	16	I want to be a successful Black woman who uses her talents to give back to the community. I want to mother many children who are not fortunate to have a motherly role model in life. I'd like to give back half of what my grandmother has given to the world.
9. Kirstie and Kristie (Twins)	16	We want to be poets and event planners.
10. Darrow	16	I feel that my purpose in life is to be on this earth to show other people who have just gone through a tough time that there is still life after death and that God does everything for a reason.
11. Dale, II	14	A pastor
12. Amaris	14	I want to be an orthodontist
13. Joy	14	Spread joy to everyone and encourage them
14. Elisha	12	To be a pediatrician
15. Charles, Jr.	11	A pastor and an engineer
16. Nathaniel, III	11	An entrepreneur, pastor, and a husband with four children
17. Bernard, Jr.	11	I'd like to become a great basketball player and make millions of dollars. I'd also like to give back to my family.
18. Jeoshua	9	A prophet, a minister, and a computer engineer
19. John	7	An entrepreneur and a minister

20. Brianna	7	To grow up and have a wonderful family and be a great mom! I also want to be a veterinarian and take care of and save many animals.
21. Joseph	6	A prophet, minister and entrepreneur.
22. Jamie	4	A veterinarian and a dentist
23. Jenesis	3	A pastor and a registered nurse

The other six grandchildren's destinies have yet to be revealed.

OUR FOURTH GENERATION

Great Grandson Bryan Hendricks II

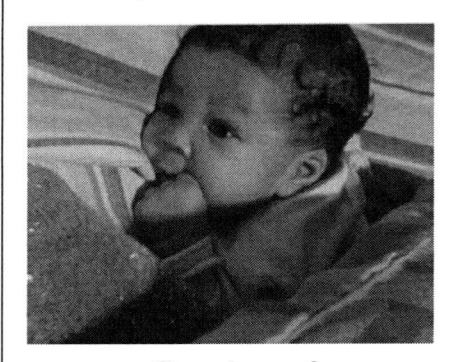

Grandson of

Bernard & Sheila Bronner

Wedding of

Christina & Bryan Hendricks

Chapter 12: Accountability

An Inheritance

From: Nathaniel H. Bronner, Sr.
To: My Children and My Children's Children

The Lord our God is one Lord: And thou shalt love the Lord thy God with all thine heart, and with all thy soul and with all thy might, (Deut. 6:4-5) and love thy neighbor as thyself.

PROVED!

Blessed is the man that feareth the Lord, that delighteth greatly in his commandments. His seed shall be mighty upon earth: the generation of the upright shall be blessed. Wealth and riches shall be in his house: and his righteousness endureth forever. (Ps. 112: 1-3)

PROVED!

Trust in the Lord with all thine heart; and lean not unto thine own understanding. In all thy ways acknowledge him, and he shall direct thy paths. (Prov. 3:5- 6)

PROVED!

God directed Grandpapa Nathaniel Bronner, Sr.'s path into the beauty trade business and blessed him with hair care products, manufacturing plants, retail stores, distribution centers, international beauty shows, annual beauty show magazine publications, Cottonwood Hot Springs, and other real estate and directed him to his wife, Grandmamma Robbie, who became his helpmate. Children: **"Remember the Lord thy God, it is he that giveth thee power to get wealth." (Deut. 8:18)**

Honor the Lord with thy substance, and with the first fruits of all thine increase: so shall thy barns (mfg. plants) **be filled with plenty, and thy presses** (vats) **shall burst out with new wine** (new products)**. (Prov. 3:9, 10)**

Grandpapa gave the seed money for Word of Faith Church, The Ark of Salvation Church, Upscale magazine and Century Systems. I have been young and now am old; I have not seen the righteous forsaken, nor his seed begging bread. (Ps 37:25) *PROVED!*

I have taught my six sons, nephews, cousins, employees, and others about the Lord. I led my six sons (Nathaniel, Jr., Bernard, Darrow, Dale, Charles, and James) to the Wheat Street Baptist Church where all were baptized under Rev. Dr. William Holmes Borders, Sr. I dedicated every store location and my home unto the Lord. *PROVED!*

[My sons] thou shalt do that which is right and good in the sight of the Lord, that it may be well with thee [Deut. 6: 18]. [Children], forget not [God's] law, but let thine heart keep [God's] commandments: Length of days, and long life, and peace, shall they add unto thee. (Prov. 3:1-2) *PROVED!*

May the grace of our Lord, Jesus Christ, be with you all, that it may be joy in your journey. Remember God's commandments to do them and teach them to your children and your children's children.

With all thanksgiving unto God in His holy heavens,
Amen and Proved!

Blessing of the Sons

A Special Thanksgiving Day Service at Our Cottonwood Hot Springs Facility

November 26, 1992

Praise and Thanksgiving

Prayer

Scripture

Holy Communion

Message: Rev. Dale Bronner

> *The Prayer of Anointing of the Father by the Son:*
> *Rev. Dale Bronner*

Lining Up of the 6 Sons

Anointing of the 6 Sons by the Father

Acceptance from Each of the 6 Sons

Gathering of All the Grandchildren

Laying on of Hands of All the Grandchildren by Grandpapa Nathaniel Bronner, Sr.

Holy Scripture in Unison (Deut. 6: 1-7)

Just as Jacob blessed each of his twelve sons before he died; Nathaniel blessed each of his six sons before he died. Mr. Bronner put his Kente cloth around his neck and blessed his children and laid hands on his grandchildren.

Note: This ceremony was held November 26, 1992. Mr. Bronner transitioned July 19, 1993.

Chapter 13: Letters from the Sons

Along life's journey, you must be thankful and grateful.

There is something about letters. Our New Testament is made up of thirteen letters, mainly from Paul that brings us into the realm of just everyday living and how to cope with it. During your journey in life, you will travel to all points of the world; but never forget your roots—that which has brought you thus far. There is a presence, a being that guides and motivates you. Take your steps swiftly, knowing that each step is ordered by God.

Lesson: What you send out is what will come back to you.

February 6, 1985

Dear Mother:

I will forever be grateful to you for the tremendous aid of love and support you have supplied to me. I can never forget the way you have gone beyond the call of duty as a mother, a wife, and a businesswoman. The labor of your love in action is unparalleled. I thank God for your loving kindness and your tender mercies. I thank God for your obedience to His Spirit, for your faith in His Word, and for your prayer life as a warrior. I thank God that He has raised you up to pray for those you are duty bound to pray for.

You are the personification of grace, of truth, and of humility. You have definitely seen that God will exalt the humble. The Lord is allowing you to see the fruits of your labor. I even heard His Spirit saying, "Surely blessing, I will bless thee, and multiplying, I will multiply thee for God is not unrighteous to forget your work and labor of love, which you have showed toward His name, in that you have ministered to the saints, and do minister!" There is resurrection power that God through Jesus awaits to bestow upon you to His glory, but I hear the voice of the Lord saying first, "Roll away the stone." I don't know what the stone is; but once it is removed, you might testify with renewed power and resurrection glory!

God has and is using you in many ways. You are one of the greatest encouragers in the world. This is why God, at times, will send you a message of encouragement. Continue to be strong in the Lord and in the power of His might!

As a child, I would always see you being a financial blessing to others; but I never dreamed that those hands that were financially blessing others would one day be such a financial blessing to me. As I have thought of your giving to me in recent months, it has brought tears of joy and thanksgiving to my eyes. As I have prayed time and time again for your giving ministry, the Lord has said, "Give, and it shall be given unto you; good measure, pressed down, shaken together, and running over, shall men give into your bosom. For with the same measure that you mete without it shall be measured to you again."

You are indeed blessed by God because of your faith and willingness to serve. You have sacrificed as a mother and a wife, but the Lord shall repay you. Because you seek no reward, it shall be given to you. The Lord shall multiply your joy. He (God) has called you as a mother of the desolate and a mother of your own. My relationship of closeness to you has been a unique one that shall never be severed. Not only have you been a mother, but also you have been a friend.

I leave you now in the spirit of love and meekness; and I bid you God's speed in Jesus name. I pray that God shall preserve you wholly and blameless until we meet at the judgment throne. I further pray that God will bring our entire household in the ark of salvation. So continue to stand for righteousness, and cry loud and spare not!!

Sincerely,

Dale

P.S. Be wary of those who continue to bring you messages in the name of the Lord. God shall lead you and He himself shall guide you in all things.

December 25, 1988

Dear Mom and Dad:

It is truly a blessing from God to have the two of you for parents. You have given us a heritage to be passed on for generations to come. With the philosophy of God first, family second, and business third—you have created a model to be replicated throughout this nation. You have succeeded in every phase of life because you first succeeded at home. You have presented to us a vast sea of knowledge, wisdom, spiritual growth, educational opportunities, and priceless values for living. These are principles that could not be learned from any school, but since our family itself is an institution, we have been exposed to these guidelines at home.

We have been given a strong backbone from a father, yet a soft touch from a mother, which have balanced to perfection in our lives. As a family with six sons, a father figure is extremely vital in the transition to manhood. We have been fortunate to have a father who has molded us into men by hard work and discipline. You are a father who has not only taught us the way with your words, but also showed us the way with your life. A God-fearing father who is available for his sons is rare, <u>yet we have one</u>! To balance the greatness of our father, a woman with the serene Spirit of God has to be on his side. A mother whose prayers have brought us over has instilled the love of God in the household. As parents, you should take great pride in knowing that God has chosen your family for His ministry which shows that He is pleased with the harmony of your blessed marriage.

As a fruit of all these elements in their proper order, you have been able to dedicate your lives to building the foundation for a prosperous business. We have been so blessed and privileged not to have to seek employment elsewhere, but to be able to contribute to the growth of our own business. Therefore, the gift of ownership stock has so much meaning because you are so willing to share such a significant part of your lives with us. The best way I can show my appreciation is to be dedicated to the perpetuation and success of our company. Thank you very much. I love you and may God continue to bless you.

Your son,
Charles

December 25, 1988

Dear Father:

The gap between our ages is great, yet through experience we have learned to understand each other. You have sometimes made me do things that did not agree with me at the moment, but through my growth in life, I now see the benefits of your will. Your wisdom has shielded me from many toils and dangers of the world—keeping me healthy and successful.

The reason I am better trained than most children is that you have shown me the way through example and not just verbally. You have equipped me with all the necessary tools to master life and to master myself. The prophet Collins said, "I will be what you have always dreamed to be." I can only accomplish that by using your principles and think and act as you behave.

You have instilled in me the ingredients of being a leader, so I can go as far as I can and bring someone else with me. The $10,000 is greatly appreciated by me, but it is worth $0.01 without knowledge of thrift. Your slogans and techniques of saving and investing are worth billions. This is the reason that I'm not concentrating my letter on the recent money, but the wisdom you have given me in handling all of my finances.

There is no other man on earth who I respect more than my father. For you have mastered the body, mind, and spirit and taught me these keys in life. You have taught me how to keep balance in everything and a system of basic priorities. May your life be long and your days fruitful.

Your son,

James

Letters From The Sons

The newsletter that follows was written to Darrow in 1992 and was found in the pocket of his car at his death in 2000. I was told how he cherished this letter. It was brought back and given to me by his cousin and best friend, Gerald Render.

MOM'S NEWSLETTER
(A monthly Individually publication for each son)
VOL 1   MAY 17, 1992

Mom's Rose

Moreover, the Lord said unto me, Take thee a great roll, and write in it with a man's pen Concerning "DARROW".

Darrow, for the first time I realize just looking at your Name -- ~~TAKE~~ the "D" off and there is the word arrow -- A slender missile weapon Consisting of a long slender shaft with a sharp pointed head, used for shooting from a bow; a mark similar in form to show direction.

God is using you to show direction to hurting people, people with unsolved solutions to their circumstances. God has given you strength of "muscle" in this walk of life -- Count in all "JOY". We don't understand life -- but we live each day asking God's guidance for the purpose of our individual walk with him. God has made you <u>tough</u> for the mission - LIVE IT! PENNED IN TEARS

You are Mom's terrific, gentle, kind, loving and strong Compassionate son -- I LOVE YOU SO MUCH! "I Love JANE" "I Love little Robbie" -- I Love "JARVIS" -- I Love Kimbely -- I Love DARROW, JR. I Love all God has added to your family! Love, Mom

12-25-88

Dear Father:

This letter is in gratitude for all of the things that you have done for all of your children, in particular me.

Our instructions were to specifically relate to the stock gift that was made to us. I realize that the stock is a major gift that should not be taken for granted. It was proper that it be pointed out to us. The stock has been gifted to us now for the past several years and we have not thought about it after leaving Merritt's (our corporate attorney).

Things can be very easily overlooked and taken for granted. I had not thought about the stock after any of the meetings. The stock gift is the semblance both real and in gesture of the transferring of the reins to a different generation. To have the foresight, the wisdom, and the denial of self to do that is tribute to the greatness of the man.

There has been instance after instance of second-generation disasters, all of which have resulted from lack of preparation and planning by the first generation. To turn over the reins to an ill-prepared second generation is as disastrous as not turning over the reins to a prepared generation.

In each case that you have described or that I have seen, improper planning or preparation has been the cause of failure or proper planning and preparation the reason for success.

After you have your job in planning and preparing, it is then up to us to carry it out. It is far easier to destroy than to build and if we do not properly carry things out, Bronner Bros. could be destroyed overnight.

It makes the gift far more meaningful knowing that the recipient both appreciates it and will respect and care for it. I give my pledge that I will give my best to Bronner Bros. I recognize that the road will not be easy, nothing worthwhile ever is. There are at least six of us; there were only two of you. There is potential for greatness.

1989 will be a challenging year. There are several things that we must do.

First, turn our financial situation around. Second, create a more communicative and harmonious atmosphere among the sons. We must begin now to set a pattern for the future. We cannot afford another year like '88 financially. Third, establish a closer relationship between you and myself.

Sometimes, we talk more, sometimes less. In '89 in addition to bringing fresh juice and water twice a month, I will be available to play golf a minimum of once a month. On the first and/or third Wednesday, I will be available to play golf each month. With six of us taking a specific day, that should give you someone to play golf with twice a week. It will do me as much good as it does you.

Everyone will not only have to work hard, but work hard doing the right things to make sure we do not repeat '88. Bronner Bros. is an institution and will survive and prosper. I shall do my part to deserve the gift, the trust, and the responsibility that has been placed upon me.

With Love and Respect,

Nate

12-25-88

Dear Daddy:

I remember the turmoil and agony of your face the day your entire family was at Attorney William Merritt's office preparing to transfer some of the company's stock into the hands of the children.

This had to be very painful from the idea of having to give to your children that which you had taken your hands to build.

One thing I can assure you of is you will always know that this company will always be your company regardless to what the stock certificate says. Trust us, because you have put in us values of God first, family second and business third. You have taught us to always be honest and to keep good company. These have been our building blocks for a sturdy foundation. You have often said, the first generation builds, the second generation enjoys, but the third generation destroys—if it is not properly nurtured. This will not be so with us, because you are not an ordinary father, nor builder, but a man who supersedes our fondest imagination. Your eyes, through the vista of time, transferred to your grandchildren an inheritance that we will keep alive in their minds, hearts and spirits.

As you groom me to one day take your place, I will uphold all the things you are teaching us and pass it on to the next generation.

Now, we thank you Daddy, for you are truly our hero.

Your son,

Bernard

Dear Mother and Daddy:

I want to thank you for the gift that you so graciously gave to me. I know that the gift is very special because it took over 40 years to make. I do want you to know that I will do everything that I can to preserve this gift. When I think about this gift, I will compare it with the parable of the talents that were given to three men: five, three, and one. Instead you gave all of us twenty. It is up to us to take this gift and use it wisely, or it will be taken away. I don't want to be the one to bury his gift, but be able to go out and double it. This gift represents a new beginning of Bronner Bros. We can only build on your shoulder what you have already begun. I understand what it stands for. I just look forward to the day when I will have the opportunity to give this gift to my children. The only difference is it will be doubled. I know the work and sacrifices you have made to make this gift possible—not only with Bronner Bros., but also in building a family. You have been there for us—through it all. Through good times and through bad times, I thank you for helping me.

Mother, I thank you for starting us off in our separate lives. I thank you for your early morning and late night prayers. I thank you for being at home when we needed you. You have eased the way when times got tough. Thanks and I love you.

To Daddy, a man of great wisdom and a listening ear, I thank you for teaching us how to be successful, but not only successful, you taught us how to raise a family. Raising six boys has not been easy, but you have done something few men have—I've never seen you smoke or drink; you came home every night, and loved your wife and children more than anything else. I love you for that! To both of you, I wish you many more years of happiness and I hope that you will continue to prosper. I know that when God does call you home, he will say, "Well done, my good and faithful servants, well done."

May God continue to Bless you,

Darrow

February 17, 1986

Dear Mother,

Grace unto you, and peace, from God our Father and the Lord Jesus Christ. I am duty-bound to thank God always for you as it is meet, because your faith grows exceedingly and your charity abounds! I thank God for your financial support to me as a minister of God. Your unalienable gift of giving from bowels of mercy and your ministries of helps have undoubtedly kept the door to receiving blessings open.

I know that you sincerely desire to do the will of God and serve Him in any capacity that He would have you to serve. I know that you have an unquenchable thirst and insatiable hunger for revelation knowledge and truth of God. I pray earnestly that you might be filled with the knowledge of His will in all wisdom and spiritual understanding. I pray that you might continue to walk worthy of the Lord unto all pleasing, being fruitful in every good work, and increasing in the knowledge of God; strengthened with all might, according to His glorious power, unto all patience and longsuffering with joyfulness giving thanks unto the Father, who has made us meet to be partakers of the inheritance of the saints in light: who has delivered us from the power of darkness, and has translated us into the kingdom of His dear Son.

I pray that God uses you more and more that your speech and preaching be not with enticing words of man's wisdom, but in demonstration of the Spirit and of powers: that your faith should not stand in the wisdom of men, but in the power of God (1 Cor. 2:4,5)!

As I write, I hear the Spirit of God saying, "Continue to Pray! Pray for things not yet revealed! Pray for leaders all over the world! Pray for your children! Pray for your business! Pray for the lost, the sick and the bound!" There is much work, yet to be done in prayer. Break tradition and deviate from the routine and listen to the voice of the Spirit so that you may pray for those who you are duty-bound to pray for. Even when you are gone to live with God, I know that I must continue your mission of prayer. I'll keep all of your children lifted up to God and I'll be a watchman over their souls. We have come from blessed seed, so we are blessed. Out of six children, three of us have a special ministerial calling – me, Nate and Charles. I've known this from high school! God used me to open a door to the ministry in our family but those who follow me will be greater than me. It pays to serve the Lord and everyday, I am encouraged the more!

There are many unimaginable things that God has in store for you. He has not even begun to exalt you as He will. God is pleased with your obedience and reverence to Him. The Lord is clearly saying to you "Call unto me, and I will answer you, and show you great and mighty things, which you don't know." God has already shown you what is good and that He requires nothing more of you but to do justly, and to love mercy, and to walk humbly with Him!

Continue steadfast in prayer for it is a powerful force! You know what it has done for you and what it can do. Sometimes, things take a while, but it is as good as done, when you pray in faith. One day George Muller began praying for five of his friends. After many months, one of them came to the Lord. Ten years later, two others were converted. It took 25 years before the forth man was saved. Muller persevered in prayer until his death for the fifth friend, and throughout those 52 years he never gave up hoping that he would accept Christ! His faith was rewarded, for soon after Muller's funeral the last one was saved!

Through the power of your prayer and faith, souls will be saved, the sick will be healed, the bound will be delivered, the lonely will be comforted! Pray on forever more in Jesus' name.

Yours in Christ,
Dale

Chapter 14: Peace in the Storm

Heart Miracle: Why We Made It

My son Nathaniel has given the best account of a set of circumstances that momentarily brought our lives to a screeching halt. Even in tragedy we must first extract the lesson to be learned and then share its benefit for the sake of others. In spite of our loss, we knew that it was our duty to sound an alarm and avoid recurrences where possible. Nathaniel retells the story:

It was an early Sunday morning when I received a 911 pager call. When I returned the call, the grim news was that my 38-year-old middle brother had just suffered what doctors believed was a heart attack. I am the president of Century Systems and also pastor of a church. It was time for Sunday school. I rushed to the hospital.

When I arrived at the hospital, my sister-in-law sat grim-faced in the waiting area as she described the events of the morning. Meanwhile, they were working on my brother in the emergency room. I knew that he had the best medical care and personal attention because two of his next door neighbors were doctors and had gone to the hospital in the ambulance with him. In less than an hour his neighbor walked past me, shaking his head. My heart sank and a cold chill like I have never felt before in my life ran through my soul. I knew without him saying that my brother was dead.

He was just 38. I was six years older. He had five children; I only have two. Other than recent high blood pressure he appeared to be in excellent health. "What happened?" I screamed inside demanding to know why such a vibrant and good soul had left.

My father had a heart attack when he was only 48. He survived. He changed his life, and he became a seeker of a more natural way of living. He taught us how to live a healthy and more natural lifestyle. Some listened more than others, but all of us live fairly health conscious lives. My father's teachings are the major reason why I had the passion with

Century Systems to help people with healthy products. My father passed at the age of 79. He was a well to do businessman. The doctors marveled at his body even at that age. His undoing was excessive stress. He outworked young men at nearly 80 and would not slow down. My mother was diagnosed with mitral valve prolapse, a congenital heart defect, and high blood pressure. She doesn't like medicine.

My parents had six sons. I am the oldest. Even with healthy lifestyles, I know genetics play a major role in health. I know the genetic weakness of the family bloodline concerning heart disease. Immediately after the death of our middle brother, my youngest brother who is my partner, began to scour the market and Internet to find the best nutritional product that would give us an edge against heart disease.

We searched and searched. No product had everything. The best one that we found required that we take EIGHT capsules a day and it still didn't have everything that we found in our research and felt we needed. We needed a product that would give us the best nutritional support for our heart, blood pressure, and cholesterol in a simple to take form. Four to eight capsules were far too many capsules to take daily. I knew my mother would not maintain that regimen. If we could not find it, we would make it. We needed it for our own family to take daily. Price was not a concern, only my family's health.

Heart Miracle™ is the result. It has the latest and the best ingredients, in a complete formula, shown to nutritionally support the heart, blood pressure, and cholesterol level in an easy to take, great tasting liquid form. It should cost $20 more per bottle but greed is a condition of the heart that we decided to fight also. We didn't skimp on the expensive ingredients such as CoQ10. I believe we will be blessed for providing such a product at such a price. Compare it to anything. As of this writing, there is nothing even close to Heart Miracle™. Your heart, just like mine and my family's, is nothing to play with.

You now see how, as a family, we could not become so overtaken by grief that we did not react responsibly to the tragedy. We investigated, made some changes, and reached out for sources of help. Finally, Nathaniel and James developed a product formulated to strengthen the heart. Based upon their research, we all began a regimen that included daily use of the product with the faith that we would not have to relive such a heart-wrenching experience. Today, thousands of individuals are on the product and are receiving vital nutrients and supplements necessary for maintenance of good health for the body in general and, more specifically, for the heart.

THE DREAM

In 1995, God gave a significant and direct dream concerning Bronner Bros. through a close friend of over twenty-five years, Evangelist Freda Slaughter, of Agape International Prayer Tower.

Walking up Martin Luther King, Jr. Drive at Ashby Street, the opposite corner of Bronner Bros., she saw a memorial garden and mentioned something about the business (Bronner Bros. Co.). I was listening very intently as she was telling the dream. There was a pause, and she repeated again, "It is just something about your business." I was silent yet listening.

In a flash, out of the dream came a vision. She said, "I see a hand!" I was screaming. She did not know Mr. Bronner had already had a hand drawn representing the five phases of the business, nor did she know that the location she saw was a plot of land Mr. Bronner had bought from the City of Atlanta to construct a museum for the beauty industry.

Then the word of the Lord came that I had to build the memorial garden as a mark of honor for my late husband, Nathaniel Bronner, Sr., who had transitioned two years prior.

The task was before me, and the vision was made clear. I knew God was directing the project. The project had to be completed before the opening of the Olympics in 1996. I had one year to get the project completed.

Habakkuk 2:2-3 was enforced and taken to another level and meaning:

> **Write the vision and make it plain on tablets, that he may run who reads it. For the vision is yet for an appointed time; but at the end it will speak and it will not lie. Though it tarries, wait for it; because it will surely come. It will not tarry.**

Today *The Hand* speaks,
and what is it in His hand?
His teachings.

THE DREAM MANIFESTED IN 1996

Making the Hand

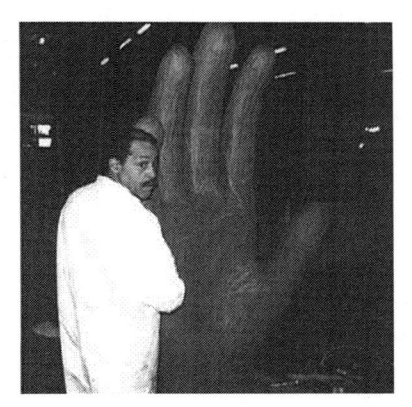

Ed Dwight, Sculptor

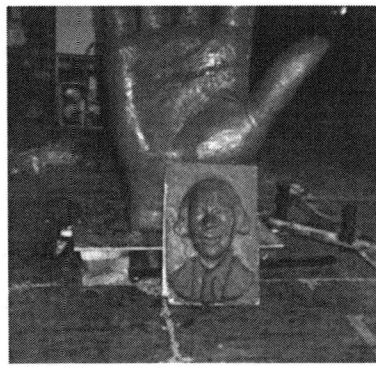

In Progress

THE HAND

THE LEGACY STATEMENT

From the Father to the Sons

From Generation to Generation
The SEEDS of Nathaniel H. Bronner, Sr.

Nathaniel H. Bronner, Sr.
Leaves a Legacy of Love
and an Uplifted Hand

To remind us to:

1. Possess the land.
2. Never cut off any fingers of the hand, no matter what your fingers may be.
3. Always remember how God led us and brought us through.
4. Teach generations to come the sacredness of the inheritance.
5. Be good stewards over what God has given us.

Never Sell Your Birthright

And the Legacy Continues....

From Grandmamma Robbie to the Grandchildren

I leave you our **faith** in God that has been lived out by our **love** through **works** in the book *Connections*.

Remember to

- Obey God, who has given us strength for the journey of life through his mercy and grace. (Read the Bible everyday.)
- Believe in our Lord and Savior Jesus the Christ, who died for our sins, our healing, and our abundant life of righteousness, peace, and joy in the Holy Spirit.
- Give thanks in everything: **"for this is the will of God in Christ Jesus concerning you. (1 Thes. 5:18)**

Follow the guide in *Connections* and all will be well with you.

The Voice within spoke,

"You have got to learn scripture."

Along my journey, I memorized

- **Psalm 91, Protection**
- **1 Corinthian 13, Love**
- **Matthew 5, Beatitudes**
- **Psalm 100, Praise**
- **Proverb 3, Instructions from a Father**
- **Psalms 1, 8, 23, 27, 46, 103, 121**

You Do Likewise! Read Psalm 145 everyday.

AN INVITATION TO THE ULTIMATE CONNECTION

"Except the Lord build the house, they labor in vain that build it." (Psalm 127:1)

At this point, you have journeyed with my family and me over the course of several decades. I have shared some of our most delicate moments. It was necessary to open up the episodes of our lives, the good and bad, so that we might serve as an example to so many others.

We have shared the ultimate winning formula—God first, Family second, and Business third. However, in order for you to align your dream with success and finally with destiny, it is necessary to first connect with the **Supreme Connector, the Lord Jesus Christ**. He is the door, the way, the truth, and the light.

Please pray this prayer with me:

Our Father,

Thank you for your Son Jesus Christ. Thank you for His death on the cross and His resurrection so that I might have eternal life. Forgive me for all my sins and cleanse me. I submit my life to you now, come into my heart.

I want to receive not only salvation but Holy Ghost empowerment to live a righteous and victorious life everyday.

Thank you Father in the name of your son Jesus, Amen.

Believe and Receive by Faith as you accept the Lordship of Jesus Christ. Read your Holy Bible daily and go to church.

CHRIST IS COMING

"Set Thine House in Order"

(2 Peter 3:10-13)

10 But the day of the Lord will come as a thief in the night; in the which the heavens shall pass away with a great noise, and the elements shall melt with fervent heat, the earth also and the works that are therein shall be burned up.

11 Seeing then that all these things shall be dissolved, what manner of persons ought ye to be in all holy conversations and godliness,

12 Looking for and hasting unto the coming of the day of God, wherein the heavens being on fire shall be dissolved and the elements shall melt with fervent heat?

13 Nevertheless we, according to His promise, look for new heavens and a new earth, wherein dwelleth righteousness.

AMEN—AMEN—AMEN!

Even in the now, we are being warned concerning global warming!

FAMILY PICTURES

Arthur E. Bronner, Sr.

Arthur Bronner, III with wife, Dr. Brenda with children and grandchildren

Elisha and Tamiko Bronner

Juanita Bronner Garmon

Rev. Dr. Reginald and Lisa Garmon with children Rachael Juanita, Brianna and baby Reginald, II.

Richard Garmon

Catherine Miller Render

G. Roland and Sherri Render with sons Jared and George, III

Gerald and Traci Render with Brooke Catherine and Gerald, Jr.

194 Connections

RUTLAND AND FOSTER FAMILIES

Prentice and Maxine Foster

The Bronner Sons and Foster Daughters
(Nathaniel, Glenda, Linda, Bernard, Darrow, Dale, Gail, Charles & James)

The Rutland, Moore and Bronner Families (Papa seated)

THE MOORE FAMILY

Maternal Grandparents
George and Roxie Moore

The Moore Sisters (L to R):
Rosa Moore, Cliffus Ferguson,
Mary Jordan and Ivester Rutland

The Moore Family Reunion,
Forsyth, GA

FAMILY AND FRIENDS

Ann Mitchell

Freda Slaughter

Janet Wallace

Dr. Juel Benson

Harriet Pitt

Delores Harmon

Gloria Dunn

Felida Neily

Mamie Bell

Devon Brown

Gloria Locke

Carolyn Mincey

HitBooks.com

Robbie Bronner CONNECTIONS
"Reflections of A Spiritual Journey"
God-Family-Business - Matriarch of the Bronner family
The How-To of rearing six successful sons and building a multi-million dollar business so you can do it too.

Nathaniel H. Bronner Jr.
FAT2Fine "The SPIRIT of Weight Loss"
The 40 Day Miracle
  "Change Your Life in 40 Days"
Quick Fasting "Easy Guide to Fasting"

Bernard Bronner
UPSCALE MAGAZINE
Published monthly
available at newstands worldwide
or subscribe at upscalemagazine.com

Darrow Bronner - Coming soon: The first book from Darrow's daughter with the gift and destiny of writing, Kimberly Bronner

Bishop Dale C. Bronner
A Checkup from the Neck Up
  "Examine Yourself"
Guard Your Gates "A Way IN & OUT"
Home Remedies "Homes In Order"

C. Elijah Bronner
7UPs, 7 Downs, 7 Turnarounds
"7 Keys to Turn Your Money Around"
Just For The Asking "Ask and Get"
How to Find God

James Bronner - BedroomTALK
"How to Turn Your Marriage Into A Lifelong Love Affair"
Learn the secrets of Love, Finance & Physical Intimacy
from the couple who had 7 kids in 10 years of marriage
BedroomTALK also available with pillow anointing oil.

This is a partial list of the Bronner books
Many books also have audio CDs at HitBooks.com